THE
LEADERSHIP
GAP

THE
LEADERSHIP
GAP

Curtis Wallace

DESTINY IMAGE® PUBLISHERS, INC.

P.O. Box 310, Shippensburg, PA 17257-0310

"Promoting Inspired Lives."

This book and all other Destiny Image, Revival Press, MercyPlace, Fresh Bread, Destiny Image Fiction, and Treasure House books are available at Christian bookstores and distributors worldwide.

For a U.S. bookstore nearest you, call 1-800-722-6774.

For more information on foreign distributors, call 717-532-3040.

Reach us on the Internet: www.destinyimage.com.

ISBN 13 TP: 978-0-7684-3973-1

ISBN 13 Ebook: 978-0-7684-8933-0

For Worldwide Distribution, Printed in the U.S.A.

1 2 3 4 5 6 7 8 9 10 11 / 13 12 11

Dedication

The Leadership Gap is dedicated to my beautiful wife, Julaina. Our partnership together and the life and family we have built are the great accomplishments of my life. If you want happiness in your life, simply marry a woman who is smarter, wiser, and funnier than you could ever hope to be.

Endorsements

"Curtis Wallace has written a tremendous resource for church, business and community leaders. Thorough, concise and engaging, this is a must read."

Jay Sekulow
Chief Counsel
American Center for Law and Justice

"Curtis Wallace lives at the intersection of faith and business. In his new book, *The Leadership Gap,* he provides the unique insight and perspective that will give you the tools you need to build and maximize a great ministry. If you are serious about going to the next level, *The Leadership Gap* is a must read!"

Tim Clinton

Contents

Foreword by T.D. Jakes

Beginning as an attorney and later as Chief Operating Officer of TDJ Enterprises, Curtis Wallace has worked alongside me for 15 years. Our work together has taken us from the construction of The Potter's House in Dallas to the world of Gospel Stage Plays and, most recently, to success in Hollywood. At the end of the day, few people can match his experience and insight when it comes to the intersection of the worlds of faith and business.

For anyone trying to build a ministry or a business, *The Leadership Gap* provides real world, practical advice that will help you get to the next level. This book is not your typical leadership book filled with inspiring platitudes written by someone who hasn't done it. Instead, you will get real solutions to real problems that you can implement now in your ministry or business.

I have a passion for transferring knowledge and taking steps to insure that we prepare the next generation of leaders in the world of faith. Curtis Wallace shares my passion and his book is a reflection of that passion. If you invest the time to read and implement the strategies in *The Leadership Gap*, you will see a return.

T.D. Jakes

Introduction

As books on leadership go, this book is unique in three respects. First, unlike most leadership books, which are written by people who either lead their organization from the top, like a CEO, or someone who are self-proclaimed "leadership expert" but don't actually have any significant operation, this book is written from the perspective of the number-two guy.

Following my legal career, I spent the last decade in the trenches serving as chief operating officer for TDJ Enterprises—the business organization of Bishop T.D. Jakes. Accordingly, my insights and observations are based on actual experiences, not theory. Additionally, my perspective as the number-two guy means that this book has specific messages for the leader of the organization as well as specific messages for the organization's staff. Third, while the book is applicable to those working in any type of business or organization with a visionary leader, it includes information specifically aimed at those individuals who are challenged with trying to grow and maximize a thriving religious organization.

The book is titled *The Leadership Gap* because I am of the opinion that far too many organizations suffer as a result of a few key gaps in the areas of people, structure, and motivation.

One of the primary goals of the book is to act as a guide or a translator. Using my experiences and the many valuable lessons I have learned during my time with Bishop Jakes, I will explain to you who are leaders what your staff isn't telling you but really wants you to know. Likewise, I share some insights with you who are staff (particularly senior executives) that will hopefully give you greater insight into your boss.

At the end of the day, remember that a small group of highly motivated individuals can indeed change the world. How do we know that to be true? Because it is the only thing that ever has.

This book will share some thoughts and truths about how your organization can build, motivate, and support that small team as it goes about its work of changing the world.

Purpose

This book exists for a singular purpose. My goal is to provide practical steps and tools to get you and your ministry over the "Leadership Gap" that is between you and real, meaningful success.

In my years of experience working with ministries, churches, and faith-related businesses, I have repeatedly observed that a few common but correctable challenges face most organizations as their leaders attempt to guide them from infancy to their potential. These mistakes and challenges create a "Leadership Gap" that the organization seems to be unable to overcome. The leader can see the promised land—the problem is that a divide that looks like the Grand Canyon (or worse, isn't seen at all) is between the organization and the success that otherwise seems so close.

The great news is that the "Leadership Gap" can be conquered. By assembling the right team of highly qualified, talented, and motivated people and by working within the proper structure and with the proper resources, you and your organization can win.

There is no time to waste on trying. The challenges faced by and the demands placed on churches and ministries have never been greater. At the same time, the opportunity has never been greater. Quite simply, it is time to get something done.

The pages that follow provide a map to help you along the way. Enjoy the ride!

From the Top

Before beginning the first chapter, I think it is important to share a couple of thoughts. First, although this book and the lessons that are shared here are meant for everyone who works in your organization, it is key that the decision to embrace the concepts and ideas set forth on the following pages comes from the top. It is up to the leader to set the tone, pace, and priorities. If something (be it embracing the concepts in this book or something as simple as starting meetings on time) is not important to the leader, it will not be important to anyone else in the organization.

As the leader, it is up to you to take the leap of faith first. The concepts set forth in this book require everyone in leadership to be honest and transparent in their assessment. That means you—the leader, the pastor, the CEO—need to be the first one to face and recognize your own weaknesses in an effort to maximize your strengths.

This book is built on the reality that no single individual can do it all—in effect, everyone, no matter how great, has *gaps*. The goal of the book is to identify how to effectively fill those gaps. By filling the gaps, you and your team will have put the puzzle pieces together; a picture will start to take shape, and results will follow.

Just as no single individual can do it all alone, it also doesn't take an army to accomplish your goals. For the vast majority of us who work in smaller organizations in business or ministry, all it really takes is the right combination of a few highly motivated and dedicated individuals. The key word in the last sentence is *combination*. If you achieve the right mix of talents and personalities, you will surely achieve something special.

Section 1

Speaking to the Leader

Chapter 1

Building the Right Team

Leadership Gap: The problem is not a lack of leaders, it is a lack of qualified, dedicated, motivated, and empowered individuals who are dedicated to supporting and making both the organization and the leader better.

In my experience, most pastors are on fairly even ground when they first start out. Everyone has his or her individual strengths—one person may be a little better preacher or a little better counselor or better teacher—but for the most part, someone who is dedicated and genuinely called to minister can start a church and attract some level of an audience. When a church is first starting out, it is simple. The pastor and his wife do it all. You answer the phone, you visit the sick, you marry and bury people, and you lead the music and preach on Sundays. To survive this stage requires energy and dedication but not much in the way of leadership skills.

As the church or ministry begins to grow and expand, the distinctions between leaders will begin to show. Why will one church grow to 5,000 in two years while another equally gifted minister is struggling to break 200? Too often the reason is clear and simple. As any organization begins to experience any level of initial success, the leader of that organization must shift and adjust to a new and different role. Now the leader needs a new set of tools to succeed. He must transform himself from the *doer* who does everything to a *leader* who acts as a visionary and executive.

For example, Steve Jobs used one set of skills when Apple was started in a garage. Jobs now uses a completely different set of skills to manage a huge multi-national corporation. The same applies to the world of ministry. What works in your living room with 10 people does not work in a mega-church with 10,000. The message that the pastor is delivering may be the same, but the methods he or she uses to manage the organization are not.

The first shift is that the leader must build a team around him or herself that can meet the demands of a growing organization. Having a quality team in place is essential to allowing the leader the freedom to focus on those areas where he or she can be most effective.

In this age of mega-churches, the career path and challenges faced by talented and anointed pastors is unlike that faced by any previous generation of pastors. When the message resonates with the congregation, growth can be, in some cases, very fast. This growth, in turn, brings a whole new set of challenges. The demands on the pastor's time and energy begin to expand exponentially (trust me, this will happen). If there is not a relief valve, two bad things happen. First, the leader becomes overwhelmed and burns out. Second, the organization's growth will stall and revert to a point where the pastor can handle the responsibility.

It is here where many ministries make their first big mistake. Maybe because they think they don't need help, or maybe because they are afraid to add overhead, or maybe because they don't know what they need, many leaders make the simple mistake of waiting too long to start building a staff. The simple truth is that no one person can do it all.

From the very beginning you should start building your team—even before you can afford a team.

So what should you do? From the very beginning you should start building your team, even before you can afford a team. When there are not sufficient resources to fund employees, work your contacts within and outside of the organization to find people who can support you on a volunteer basis. Put together a board of quality individuals—people who have experience and contacts you don't yet possess. Network and identify mentors, both from the ministry as well as the business worlds, to help guide and point you in the right direction. Think in terms of people who can not only help you now but into the future as well. Then, as the church begins to grow and income becomes sufficient, these same relationships can help you in the process of building out a paid staff.

THE RIGHT STAFF

Once you are ready, the question is who do you hire? What skill sets do you need? What types of personalities work? There are a myriad of questions to be answered.

As a beginning point, my view is that the pastor needs to think in terms of building two separate teams. One team is the ministry team. Most pastors are really good at this side of the equation, so I will direct my comments toward the other team that the pastor needs to build—the team that manages the day-to-day business affairs of the church.

While we live today in an exciting era filled with mega-churches and often rapid growth, the reality is that very few ministers have any training, expertise, or inclination in the areas of leadership, management, and business skills. At the same time, any growing, successful ministry now has needs and challenges ranging from human resources to real estate to IRS compliance to governmental relations to finance. It is in dealing with the demands and complexities of this world where most pastors fall short, and for good reason. The ability to effectively preach and manage a large business organization rarely comes in the same package (in fact, I work for the only person I have ever met who can do both).

The need then becomes pretty clear. As the organization that is the church grows, the pastor needs to put in place a team with the talent, experience, and expertise required to manage that organization.

The pastor needs a team with the talent, experience, and expertise to manage the organization.

The problem is that as many pastors start building their staffs, they make the understandable mistake of only focusing on the ministry side of the organization and only hiring people who look, think, and act like they do. Most good pastors are generally creative extroverts who need to talk to and guide and lead people—and that is great. However, the result of hiring a group of people who meet the pastoral requirement is a team of "pastors" who will be looking for their own ministry group to lead, oversee, and inspire (correctly so—they want a group of people to pastor). At the end of the day, you end up with one "pastor," who leads the overall organization, supported by a staff of people who all perceive themselves as ministry leaders who will oversee their individual area where they get the individual satisfaction that they need to be fulfilled as a minister.

That gets you halfway to the finish line. It doesn't get you to the finish line. With the right ministry staff, you will have a group of inspired ministries under the aegis of a group of fulfilled leaders. The problem is that it leaves no one to focus on the details of running the business side of an organization. There is no one who focuses on making the organization the best it can be.

The second mistake that all too many leaders make, then, compounds the first when they assign one of their ministry leaders to take the role of executive pastor or administrator. The problem here is that you have someone who has a great heart for ministry but no business skills (or worse yet, perceived business skills) running the business side of the organization.

To solve the problem, the pastor, at the same time that he or she is building out the pastoral staff, needs to be giving even greater focus toward building a team with disparate talents and disparate callings to lead the business of the organization.

PEOPLE WHO UNDERSTAND WHERE THEY FIT

When the leader embarks on the process of building the team, it is important to focus on a few key points. First, one key to success in any organization, but certainly with a church or ministry, is for the leader to build a team where everyone involved in leadership understands his or her 1) respective gifts and talents, 2) weaknesses, and 3) roles within the organization. God has graced each of us with specific talents that need to be used and maximized. Likewise, we all have weaknesses that need to be managed as well. It is our responsibility to use those gifts and talents. With an understanding of each person's talents, the team can be organized in a way where people are in the right role. Remember, the most talented person in the world cannot fully succeed in the wrong role—it will only lead to frustration on all sides.

**The most talented person in the world
cannot fully succeed in the wrong role.**

In the church today, one of the hardest things to find, and one of the most valuable, is people who embrace the fact that their calling and talent is best suited for a role that supports and makes the pastor or leader more effective. That is the role that I perform. As COO of TDJ Enterprises, my job is to effectuate the goals set forth by our leader, Bishop T.D. Jakes, as he has been directed by God. One of the reasons that I took this position was that while working as a lawyer to many of the country's top ministries, I witnessed a surprising lack of talent among the management ranks of many organizations. What I observed is what I referenced above—the business side of many ministries was being run by really great, well-intentioned people with a heart for ministry but who were simply out of their league in a large, complex ministry organization.

THE GOAL IS TO FREE THE PASTOR

While I like to do some of things that Bishop Jakes does so well, such as speaking or writing, I recognize that I do not possess the gifts he has been given for ministry leadership. I do, however, possess gifts and talents that Bishop Jakes needs in order to become as effective as possible. Simply put, at the end of the day, no one can do it all. Responsibilities have to be divided and delegated. That means that my job (and what every ministry needs) is to lead a team of people who are dedicated to the same objective—our efforts *free* Bishop Jakes to focus on leading and doing what he is called to do—minister to the masses.

This point cannot be overemphasized. No pastor or leader, no matter how anointed or talented, can reach his or her full potential if he or she is burdened with trying to manage all of the myriad details that must be tended to in a large organization. I have said it before, but this single issue can be the one thing that holds back potentially great leaders.

The pastor/leader needs to understand his or her role and then find a team that allows him or her to effectively fulfill that role. You can't break beyond being a storefront church if you continue to operate like a storefront. The pastor needs to focus on his or her gifts and talents and then find a team of people who share his or her vision but also possess the skills needed to fill in the gaps where the pastor is either weak or doesn't have the time to be involved.

You can't go beyond being a storefront church if you continue to operate like a storefront.

This requires everyone, particularly the pastor, to be honest about what his or her gifts are. In my years of working with ministries, I have met very few pastors who actually possess any meaningful business skills. My apologies to all of the great pastors I have met and worked with over the years, but this is too important for anything but brutal honesty and reality. Unfortunately, another truth is that too many pastors (because they are born leaders who believe the ability to lead equals the ability to manage) believe that they are the ministry's equivalent of Donald Trump, Warren Buffett, and Bill Gates all wrapped up in a preacher's suit. I don't mean to be derogatory or disparaging. I am simply trying to articulate what I have observed. The great thing is that a pastor/leader does not need to be Bill Gates to succeed. You simply need to hire a team that does in fact possess the requisite skills. Once you do that, you will be ready to move to the next level.

Too many pastors believe the ability to lead equals the ability to manage.

WHAT TO LOOK FOR IN SENIOR BUSINESS STAFF

If you are like most pastors, the most important position(s) for you to fill are those one or two senior executives who manage the major elements of your organization. For example, with Bishop Jakes, I am COO of TDJ Enterprises, and I manage all of Bishop Jakes' for-profit business interest. Likewise, I have a counterpart who acts as COO of The Potter's House and manages the nonprofit ministry. In turn, both myself and my counterpart at The Potter's House are each supported by a chief financial officer who manages the financial matters of their respective organization. Having these two executives in place will give you the foundation that you need to build out the entire team. Effectively, everyone else on the executive team will report to these two individuals who, in turn, will report to the leader.

You will find that having a senior executive team in place will not only free up the pastor's time to focus on ministry issues, but it also gives the pastor an all-important buffer. What I mean here is that the pastor should almost never be the conveyer of bad news. However, effectively running any organization means making choices and setting priorities. Any time priorities are set and choices are made, usually someone wins and someone loses (or least perceives him or herself to have won or lost). The choir is upset because they think they didn't get new robes because the youth got new video games. The accountant thinks that the extra income from last month should be placed in savings, but someone else thinks that the sound equipment needs to be updated. Management is choices. It is the job of the buffer/executive to explain the choices to the leaders of the various groups that make up the church.

The pastor should almost never be the conveyer of bad news.

Similarly, because the pastor has a dual role of employer/boss and pastor for the employees, he or she should not be doing the firing or other disciplinary actions. The pastor needs to stay out of the trenches and above the fray as much as possible. I don't mean to imply that the pastor should not take responsibility—he or she should. But the pastor also needs to remain in a place where he or she can maintain relationships and focus on the big picture.

So the goal is to find the right individual(s), someone who shares the vision but also has a background and talents completely different from yours. Here are some of the attributes that I think you should be looking for when seeking your go-to person.

THE BASICS

In the course of finding the right person, you will, naturally, look at the typical factors. Educational backgrounds and prior work experience are of course very important. Remember that everyone is a result of the sum total of his or her experiences. You need to consider the total person.

Being a lawyer, I am admittedly biased, but I do think that a legal education and background can be very helpful for someone running a ministry. The reason is that lawyers are trained to collect and analyze information, pros and cons, and then make a decision. In other words, law school is all about learning to think. Those analytical and critical thinking skills can be applied to any industry or situation. (This is why so many non-practicing lawyers end up as Fortune 1000 CEOs, successful entrepreneurs, and Hollywood executives.) If you do hire a lawyer or former lawyer, look for those whose background is in the business/deal-making side and not as a litigator. The reason is that litigators are trained to be confrontational and to fight, whereas business lawyers are trained to find a way to get things done and to solve disputes, not create them.

Regardless of whether you choose to hire someone with a legal background, a business background, or something else, here are a few key points to consider.

HIRE SENIOR EXECUTIVES
WHO SPEAK MULTIPLE LANGUAGES

I am not talking about Spanish or Mandarin Chinese. I am talking about the ability to seamlessly transition and flow between diverse settings and circumstances. While my work is not typical of what most ministry executives experience, it is a useful reference. During any one week, my work may take me from a formal dinner meeting with the Governor of Texas to meeting with a group of high-profile pastors about a new business opportunity, to a board of directors' meeting for a company that we own a stake in, to a creative meeting with executives at Sony Pictures about a film project, to negotiating a real estate deal. Every day brings a diverse group of people who I need to be capable of communicating with and understanding. To do that effectively, I have to be fluent in the "language" that is being used by my audience. The point is simple—I cannot do my job if I cannot flow between these diverse settings and adjust to the language spoken at each.

Think of it as being similar to doing business internationally. There is one set of rules and customs for doing business in Japan and another for doing business in South Africa. You wouldn't attempt to do business in these diverse areas without a team who could flow between them and understand the distinctions, so why do so with your ministry?

So as you build out your staff, consider the multitude of situations in which your staff may need to be able to effectively function. Also, remember that the diversity of the situations will increase as the complexity and size of your organization expands. In today's modern mega-church, the senior staff executives need to be able to function in a wide variety of areas. This means not only being comfortable in whatever the setting is (from a formal dinner to a casual business lunch to a revival) but being fluent in the language that the setting and the people require. Your team will not be effective if they can only speak and act like they do on Sunday morning. I am not talking about being something you are not; I am talking about being flexible and knowing and adapting to your audience.

Your team will not be effective if they only speak and act like they do on Sunday morning.

For example, if your team is meeting with a bank about a multi-million dollar loan for a new facility and the banker wants to know how you know you can repay the loan, answering that you have faith and God will provide will not get you the loan. You need to know what your audience (a banker in this case) wants to discuss and how he or she is accustomed to receiving that information. In the case of a banker, he or she is looking for spreadsheets, charts, and graphs that explain (in his language) things like how much money the congregation has already pledged toward the project, what the church's budget looks like, what is the income history, and how the church's free cash flow is more than sufficient to service the debt. The banker wants to see evidence of financial accountability and responsibility—not evidence of faith.

One of the things that Bishop Jakes and I often say about each other is that we act as translators for each other. When I first started with Bishop Jakes, we were producing the *Woman, Thou Art Loosed* stage play. At one of our first stops on the tour, I was the only white guy for five miles. I was completely out of my element. The venue was run by some less than reputable people who clearly intended to not pay our company the money we were owed after a very successful week of shows.

On Saturday, Bishop Jakes had to leave to fly back to Dallas to preach at The Potter's House on Sunday. Before he left, he interpreted the situation for me. He wisely pointed out that the people we were working with would try to push me around. He said, "Don't get mad, because if you do, you can't win the fight with these people." He said, "Be who you are. If you act like a lawyer and get technical with them, you will take them out of their element and you can win." Bottom line—I came back home with the money and have now been with Bishop Jakes for ten years. The point is that I needed a translator in this instance.

In other cases, the scenario has been switched, and I have been able to interpret people and situations for Bishop Jakes. Bishop Jakes and I have been able to turn the fact that we are from different worlds and have different experiences into a positive thing. We complement each other. The point is that your people must be able to flow in a multitude of situations and be able to complement each other.

FIND TRUTH-TELLERS

Another vital characteristic in a senior executive is the ability to tell truth to power. At first blush, you probably think of course my staff is honest—and they are. The issue is the ability to respectfully disagree with the leader and be able to articulate why.

One of my favorite television shows is *The West Wing.* (If you haven't seen it, it is about the interactions of the president of the United States and his senior staff.) In the show, it is very common for the senior staff to debate the merits of a particular course of action in front of the president. The president then uses that input and debate (pro and con) in making his decision. Oftentimes, that debate involves taking a position you believe to be right, knowing that the president likely disagrees. In one great episode, a new member of the staff was sent into the Oval Office to discuss some action that he was told the president wanted to take, but which the new staff member knew was the wrong thing to do. In reality (or the reality of the show), the president didn't want to take the proposed course of action. The entire exercise was a test to see if the new guy on staff would tell the president he was wrong. That is telling truth to power. Your staff is useless if they won't do it. You need independent thinkers who will contribute to the dialogue and debate and help the organization's leader find the right answer.

———◆•◆•◆———

**You need independent thinkers who will
help the leader find the right answer.**

———◆•◆•◆———

Just as important as truth telling to power is the ability of your staff to have the debate and when it is over and the decision has been made, for everyone to say, "Great, let's go get it done!" without any feelings about who won or lost the debate. It is not about winning or losing or personal agendas. It is about a team all contributing the value of their expertise to assist a leader in making the final decision.

If your people have a hard time embracing decisions they didn't make or decisions they didn't agree with, you are going to have a management problem. While management by consensus can be effective, at the end of the day decisions have to be made, respected, and acted upon. The goal, at the end of the day, is results. The success of the team and the results achieved by the team are far more important than bruised egos.

RELATIONSHIP BUILDERS

In addition to the ability to speak multiple languages and tell truth to power, seek out senior staffers who excel at building relationships and alliances both within and outside of the church. One of the most valuable things that my counterparts and I bring to the table is the value of our contacts and relationships, many developed over years of work. That list of a few thousand names and numbers in my iPhone has significant value. To build those relationships required a significant commitment and investment of time and energy.

Moreover, if your people are good at building relationships, it also means that they know how to treat people well. This is hugely important. To begin with, your staff is a reflection of you. If your team treats people badly, the people your organization works with will make similar assumptions about you and your organization. In addition, if your staff mistreats people, you will constantly have to rebuild and start over relationships—something that requires time, money, and effort to accomplish. Worse, sometimes it is not even possible to reverse the damage done by team members who do not know how to treat people.

Your staff is a reflection of you.

More than once, we have had employees with tremendous ability and talent, but they simply thought it was OK to treat people badly. The results are always disastrous and end the same way. Once you figure out what is happening, you have to fire the employee and then spend a lot of time fixing things in order to be able to effectively do business and repair your reputation.

Having a team that treats people well and excels at building quality business relationships will pay off in a number of concrete ways. First, you will enjoy the benefits of quality, long-term business relationships. It is simply much easier and cheaper to do five deals with one partner than to do five separate deals with five separate partners. In business partnerships, like other relationships, a great deal of effort goes into getting to know each other and developing a level of trust and mutual respect. Having to constantly repeat that process is time-consuming and expensive.

Another benefit of relationship building is that when you do embark on a new initiative or project, more often than not you will not be starting from ground zero. Instead, as you start the new project, your team can lean on their collective relationships and contacts. You will often find that someone on your team has a relationship that can add value or assist in some way with what you are trying to accomplish.

Having senior executives who build relationships will aid the process of freeing the pastor/leader. One of the recurring themes of this book is that the organization's leader needs to be free from the daily grind of minutiae and making the trains run on time to focus on the issues of most importance to the organization. Generally, that means that the leader should focus on building and maintaining only very high-level relationships. This means that the senior staff needs to focus on all of the other relationships that are required for success.

Interestingly, in many cases it is actually the lower staff-level relationships that can actually get more done. For example, the pastor may be friends with the mayor of your city, and that relationship can be a great way to start if you are trying to get something done with the city. In reality, however, it is the relationship of your senior execs with the high-level city staff (the people who actually do things as opposed to the politicians) that will be crucial to getting the project or request through the red tape and to the finish line. Mayors, like CEOs and other high-profile people, tend to avoid getting specific; the staff will tell you the real deal.

A similar philosophy applies to business as well. At TDJ Enterprises, we are in the movie business and have a great partnership with Sony Pictures. At Sony, Bishop Jakes has developed a personal relationship with the chairman and CEO of Sony Pictures. Bishop Jakes and Michael Lynton focus their attention on matters at the highest level in the relationship, like what movies we are going to make. At the same time, Derrick Williams (one of my colleagues at TDJ Enterprises) and I have built great relationships with other executives at Sony Pictures, like Devon Franklin (make sure that you check out his book, *Producing by Faith*), and together we focus on executing the vision set forth by Bishop Jakes and Michael Lynton. You need partners and advocates at every level to reach the level of success you are reaching for.

You need partners and advocates at every level to attain the success you are reaching for.

Building good relationships is also important for information gathering. In order to make good decisions and effectively negotiate, you need good information. That information comes from people. You need good relationships with the right people to get good information. The more people within your given industry areas you know and call on, the higher the quality of the information that you can get.

Here is an example from a recent planning meeting that I was involved in. We were discussing future events and identifying potential host cities for the events. When we put on a large event, we don't pick cities at random. We consider everything from climate to hotels to airport capacity and, naturally, how aggressive the city is going to be in attracting our business. We also consider the relationships we have in each city—with the government, with other faith organizations, and with business leaders. We are looking for every edge we can get, and relationships are a big part of that. Similarly, because so many senior staffers on our team are well connected, we know the industry trends, we know what cities are being aggressive—who, for example, has been actively chasing our business. You see, starting at square one is simply too hard to do every time—information and relationships will take you well down the road to success.

Finally, I also believe that your organization needs to be conscious of diversity in hiring. Diversity can pay significant dividends. The world is becoming increasingly diverse, and your organization can benefit from it as well. For example, as a high-profile white guy in a largely black organization, it is common for other white people we are dealing with to work to build a bond with me because they are comfortable with me (that is a topic for another book). That gives me an advantage, because I find out what they are really thinking. Also, everyone outside of your organization who has a conversation with the pastor/leader is generally going to be reserved and hold back, whereas in many cases the same people will let loose with staff. Use it to your advantage.

So as you build the team, look beyond academics and experience to the intangibles of people who are multi-lingual, comfortable across a variety of settings, will tell truth to power, and know how to build and maintain relationships.

CLOSE THE GAP

1. Describe the timing and importance of a leader's shift from being a *doer* to a *leader.* Are any "shift delays" limiting your organization's growth?

_____

_____

_____

_____

2. How many teams does a church or ministry need to function effectively? Why isn't a ministry team enough? How can a better understanding of this balance improve your organization?

_____

_____

_____

_____

3. Every team member must understand his or her talents, gifts, weaknesses, and role. What are the dangers of not recognizing or accurately assessing these elements? How well-defined are yours?

_____

_____

_____

_____

4. Explain the leader's need for a buffer. What is at risk when no buffer exists? How well is this kind of buffer functioning in your organization?

_____

_____

_____

_____

5. What is the importance of hiring those who speak multiple "languages"? How deep is your organization's bench in this regard? Which "languages" could be better represented?

_____

_____

_____

_____

6. Explain the importance of hiring independent thinkers who are willing to speak truth to power. When is it time to stop debating and move forward? Can you identify any bottlenecks that may be hindering your organization in these areas?

_____

_____

_____

_____

7. How would you rate your organization's relationship-building? Is it occuring at all levels? Are you satisfied that all team members represent the organization well? What deficiencies need to be addressed?

_____

_____

_____

_____

Chapter 2

Motivating and Inspiring the Team

Leadership Gap: Even with a great team in place, the organization will not achieve its potential until the leader learns to effectively motivate and inspire the team.

Now you have built a great team. The next step is to effectively motivate and inspire them to reach beyond themselves to achieve more than either they or you thought possible. However, before discussing any specifics about how I think that a pastor should approach motivating the team, I think it is important for most pastors to understand something foundational about themselves.

THE PASTOR MUST UNDERSTAND AND ADAPT TO THE REALITY OF HIS DUAL ROLE

One unique reality of churches is that the pastor plays a dual role when it comes to most of the organization's staff. For the most part, the pastor is not only the leader and boss of the organization; he is also the spiritual leader of the same staff members. The reality of this dual role leads to a couple of implications that need to be properly understood.

First, because the pastor is the spiritual leader of the staff, it can be very difficult for the staff to question or challenge the pastor. This goes back to the issue pointed out in Chapter 1 about the ability of key staff to tell truth to power. So, based on that suggestion, hopefully the organization has at least hired senior people who are willing to tell truth to power. However, just as important as having a strong staff who will tell truth to power, the pastor needs to be aware of this issue and create an atmosphere of openness that encourages staff to say what they really think. The leader and only the leader can create that atmosphere.

If the leader is not actively seeking to create the open atmosphere that is needed, it will not happen on its own. Unless the pastor actively and positively responds to opinions and ideas that do not line up with his, the staff will over time stop offering those opinions. People, for the most part, have strong survival instincts and will begin to act in a way that does get them positive reinforcement (or at least no negative reinforcement).

Worse, the best of your staff will, over time, begin to make their exits if an open atmosphere does not exist. Remember, all good executives have options. Absent an atmosphere that lets them contribute in a meaningful way, they will find a new home. At that point, the downward spiral will begin—as the good people leave, you are left with only the weak who don't care about input because they don't have any to offer in the first place.

--------◆•◆•◆--------

**Without an atmosphere that lets them
contribute in a meaningful way, executives
will find a new home.**

--------◆•◆•◆--------

In addition to making the staff less than objective about the pastor and reluctant to question or disagree, it can also make the pastor less than objective about the staff. As a pastor, your inclination is to love, embrace, protect, and help the flock. Just as a parent may not see the weaknesses of his child, a pastor may not see the weaknesses of his staff.

I have often heard Bishop Jakes talk about how he has debates between the two sides of his brain. The side that is a pastor wants to embrace and love and fix the problems that an employee may be having. At the same time, the side of his brain that is a business man wants to take action and tell the problem employee to shape up or ship out.

The point is that the pastor needs to have enough self-awareness to understand his or her own internal conflicts and act accordingly. If you know that your pastoral instincts generally rule the day, you need to take compensating steps. Make sure that you have someone on staff who can make the distinctions and works closely with you to make these tough calls.

This pastor/businessperson conflict often becomes pronounced in times of economic difficulties. During the recent (and some say ongoing) recession, churches all over the country were forced to deal with the combined realities of large drops in charitable giving at a time of an unprecedented increase in demand for services. Compounding the problem for most churches was the simple fact that most churches were far too slow to react to the crisis. All too often, one reason for slow response was the leaders' unwillingness to make tough decisions and reduce staffing levels in a time of economic crisis. The pastoral instinct kicked in, and the pastor delayed action because of his or her desire to protect and help people.

The result of the delay in acting is generally that the number of people eventually hurt by the cuts grows with time. In many cases a small reduction in overhead made early can prevent a much larger cutback taken later on.

A third implication of the pastor's dual role is that staff are often so eager to please and show loyalty that they will overreact to statements made by the pastor. What happens is that something said in passing is interpreted as an edict from on high. The most common refrain heard throughout the organization is "Pastor said…." It is used to justify anything and everything, and too often the pastor either didn't even say it at all or, if he or she did, it was misinterpreted.

Here is a simple example. Suppose the pastor may be looking a sample postcard mailer designed to promote an upcoming sermon series and he says something along the lines of, "You know what? Maybe we should use a yellow font instead of a blue font color." The next thing you know, one statement about the color scheme of one postcard becomes an edict that gets passed down through the ranks that the pastor doesn't want to use any more blue fonts ever and only wants to use to yellow— forever and ever amen. Pastors need to understand that the simplest statement about something seemingly insignificant can easily be wildly overblown, just in an effort to please the pastor, thus the need for exceptional clarity from the pastor.

Obviously, when you are the leader, you want your team to take what you say to heart and act on it. However, you do not want your staff misinterpreting you or taking a passing comment and making it into something bigger. Because the staff is likely to take so seriously what you say, you just need to be careful and clear.

So, the first step toward properly motivating your team is to recognize the pastor's dual role and take appropriate steps to compensate. The leader needs to encourage open and truthful debate and dialogue among senior staffers, recognize when the pastor side of the brain is incorrectly creating problems for the business side of the brain, and be exceedingly clear in his or her instructions to the staff.

THE MOTIVATIONAL EDGE

The great thing about working with a church staff is that, on a certain level, motivation is easy. The people, for the most part, have joined the staff because they want to be a part of the broader meaning and significance that working in a religious organization can provide. Unlike a career in a law firm or a large corporation, where satisfaction comes from the quality of the work and making money, there is a larger purpose at work here. Great church staffers are responding to a higher calling. The result is that your staff should largely be "pre-motivated." Now you just need to harness that motivation and point it in the right direction.

An important point here—just because the staff is "pre-motivated" doesn't mean that the leader can ignore this area. Just because I have a built-in desire to do well and achieve results doesn't mean that I am not human. I still want the same things every employee wants. I still want to be paid well. I want to receive recognition when it is due. The simple reality is that when people do well, they should be noticed. It is not difficult and it is free, but the results of it are priceless.

When people do well, they should be noticed. It is not difficult and it is free, but the results are priceless.

A friend of mine, Louis Upkins, recently wrote a great book (I highly recommend it) called *Treat Me Like a Customer*. After working with countless successful businessmen who were losing their families and had horrible private lives (despite being great people—these are guys who attend church, don't cheat on their wives, etc.), he saw a common thread. These guys were investing more time in their customers and treating them better than their families. By simply advising these men to treat their families as good as their best customers, families have been saved. The same rule applies to employees. You need to treat your employees as well as you treat your biggest giver. Do that and see what kind of results you get.

In order to be effective, the staff must be empowered.

Lots of ministers spend a huge amount of time and effort telling their congregations about how to be empowered in their lives financially, spiritually, and otherwise. However, too many churches fail to adequately empower their own teams. It is "Management 101" that people who are not empowered are not effective. People need to feel like they are empowered to act (within certain boundaries) if they are to be at their best. Every job, no matter how low on the totem pole, needs to involve some level of discretion—I may be sweeping the floors, but I should be the one deciding how to best sweep the floors as long as I can get it done with excellence.

As you move up the ladder to senior leadership, the level of discretion should increase with the level of the employee and his or her track record.

The problem that all too many leaders face is that they do not know how to let go. They want to make every decision and solve every problem. Oftentimes this need to control has roots in the fact that as he or she was starting out, the pastor by necessity had to do everything because there was no one else. The pastor became accustomed to doing it all. Then as the organization grew and staff was added, the pastor's instincts took over and he or she didn't use the staff he or she had.

When the leader micromanages and makes all of the decisions, the staff has no say and no power. As a result, two things happen. First, the good people will leave. If I can't use my brain, I will not be fulfilled as a person and I will go somewhere where I get that fulfillment. The next thing that will happen is nothing. The remaining staff will not act. Why? Because there is no incentive for them to do so.

Time and time again, I have gone in to advise churches only to find that everything pointed back to the pastor. No one had any authority, and as a result, no one really did anything. Everyone simply waited for the pastor to make a decision, and a huge bureaucratic bottleneck was created. No one felt empowered to make a decision without having the boss on board.

I recognize that there needs to be a balance here. Clearly, as the leader you need and want to be informed, updated, and in the loop. However, there is a difference between being informed and making every decision. Your executives should be telling you what they are doing and why (and you have the prerogative to reverse them if you disagree), but they should be *doing*, not waiting for you. If your top executives will not act, why have them? If your staff just brings you problems to solve, why have them?

As part of this process, you will need to develop with your most senior team members clear delineations of power. Obviously, all really big decisions need to be decided on the leader's desk. The critical word here is *big*.

Your staff needs to keep everything other than significant decisions off your desk. As the leader, it is your job to give direction and then send your team off to implement. Then those items that come to your desk should be only the most important and complex organization-impacting decisions. And those should be made with significant input from the staff.

As the leader, it is your job to give direction and then send your team off to implement.

Early on, during one of our stage play tours, my boss did me a great favor. He got up in front of the staff and explained that if I told them something, I was speaking for him. It is my job to keep him in the loop on what I do and what I am planning. But it is also my job to make decisions and get things done. T.D. Jakes sets the goal and the vision. How I choose to get to the destination is largely my decision and my call.

Over time, the team gets a good feel for what the boss wants to have input on and what he or she wants the staff to just do. With clear lines of communication and a little time and trust, everyone will develop a good sense of where the proper lines are.

One additional and related problem occurs when the leader holds too much power—the staff will have a tendency to only bring problems to the pastor for him or her to solve. Again, why have staff if that is all that they do? Tell your staff that when they bring you a problem to also bring their ideas for solving the problem. You want to develop a staff that takes the initiative and brings solutions along with the problem. You want a team that offers fresh perspective and contributes meaningfully to critical discussions.

As I mentioned previously, one of my favorite television shows is *The West Wing*. It stars Martin Sheen and is about how the president and his senior staff interact. It offers great lessons in leadership and how a team should work together to achieve a common purpose. Lively discussions are an ongoing happening as staff members debate and argue for their positions. The point is not to fight but to try to find the right or at least the best answer you can. Just as the issues that get resolved by the president and his staff are, by definition, some of the world's biggest problems, the issues that get resolved by the senior pastor and his senior staff are likewise the biggest issues facing the church. If the decisions are easy, the lower level staff are not doing their job.

Like the staff of *The West Wing*, you want your staff to be able to argue and debate and problem-solve, all without taking it personally. If two of your top staffers can't have an argument over a course of action and then go to lunch happy, they are not right for the job. Real senior executives can separate the two things. They recognize that just because someone else has a different idea doesn't mean that it is a bad idea. This includes the ability to debate and discuss options with the boss. Your staff must be able to articulate what they think.

———◆———

Real senior executives recognize that a different idea doesn't mean a bad idea.

———◆———

In a great episode of *The West Wing*, one of the president's senior advisors, Sam Seaborn (played by Rob

Lowe), was attracted to and wanted to date the daughter of the chief of staff, Leo McGarry. Leo decided to have a little fun and gave his daughter, a public school teacher and a staunch advocate of public schools, a position paper that Sam had written advocating a school voucher program. The chief of staff's daughter, Mallory, was incensed and started a fight with Sam. Only later did she learn that Sam didn't agree with the position paper—he had just written it to argue the other side in the internal debate about the issue going on in the White House. The point is that you need the smart people to look at and discuss every side before you can make a good decision.

**The Church needs to be willing to pay for
top talent to get top talent.**

This seems to be one of those taboo subjects in the world of church administration, so I am going to address it head-on. I think it is pretty clear from the above that I advocate putting together a small team of a few highly placed executives in place to help the leader run the organization. It is also clear that the executives need to be high-quality (just think about who they need to interact with). The result is that you need a great team. To get that, you need to pay for it. People who serve in faith-based organizations all share the common element of a true desire to help advance the vision. However, that altruistic feeling will not replace, over the long term, some degree of financial success and reward.

Remember this—all good executives have options and usually plenty of them. You don't want people who don't have the ability to go elsewhere. Recently, Bishop Jakes and several of the leadership team from The Potter's House and TDJ Enterprises conducted a seminar at a large church for a group of pastors and leaders. Bishop Jakes explained to his fellow pastors that he knew that any of his senior staff could leave at any time to go do something else. This is true because the team is so high-quality. It also means that we are where we are because we want to be there. Finally, it means that Bishop Jakes doesn't have to feel like his team is dependent upon him; we are not.

So find the team, empower the team, and pay the team fairly. Setting salaries should be the result of informed decision-making. You need to obtain quality information on salary levels for comparable organizations in your area. Apply that information and build in incentives and you will be well on your way.

Remember, you only need a few highly compensated executives to make your organization run well. After all, it only takes a few highly dedicated individuals to change the world. How do we know this is true? Because it is the only thing that ever has.

The bottom line is that you don't need a big team. Even the largest faith-based organization can be effectively managed with a pastor/leader and two to four really good senior executives—everyone else are the subordinates who do the actual work based on the vision and direction of the senior team.

Having too many managers can bog down an organization as fast as not having enough. In my view, a quality, faith-based organization can be run effectively with a CEO/pastor, a chief operations officer to run the business operations, a chief financial officer to manage finances, and an associate to run the pastoral staff. Everyone else should be part of the teams that report to these people. On the next level, the senior executives should then each have a team reporting to them. Also, the organization should be relatively "flat," with a minimum of "middle management" who simply take what their boss says and convey it to their subordinates. Everyone should meaningfully add to the organization.

———————•◦•◦•———————

Churches need to avoid "thumb-sucking."

———————•◦•◦•———————

Part of motivating any team is actually doing something. Organizations that get stuck in paralysis by analysis—or worse, a simple inability to create the inertia needed to act—will drive good people away. People, especially cause-oriented people, want to see things happen in a deliberate manner. People want to be associated with winners who are moving forward—not organizations dying a slow death.

A related issue arises with regard to problem people. The simple fact is the greatest executive in the world may not be suited to be a member of your team. A team has to be just that—a team. In some cases, a great executive doesn't want to be a part of a team and needs to go do his or her own thing. In other cases, personal issues, integrity issues, outside distractions, etc., can get in the way of good employees acting that way. However it happens, problem employees are a big issue. The problem too often is worsened by an organization that sucks its thumb instead of doing something about it.

I subscribe largely to the Jack Welch views on employment. A significant part of a leader's time should be used identifying, developing, and motivating good employees. Oftentimes, when an employee is not a fit in a particular job, the organization should make every effort to find the right situation for that employee—either within or outside of the organization. Also, leaders need to be clear with employees about how they are doing. This is hugely difficult to do. But we owe it to our employees.

However, when it becomes clear that an employee does not fit and is not a valued member of team (for whatever reason), act quickly and decisively. It is all too easy to put on the pastor's hat, hug the employee, and hope things get better. They rarely do.

I recently read a biography on Warren Buffet called *Snowball*. In the book, it was clear that Buffet hated confrontation and hated firing people. He is known for buying companies with good managements and letting them run the business. However, good management occasionally goes bad. Buffet learned the hard way a few times that "thumb-sucking" (doing nothing and hoping a problem goes away) does not work. It is best to act quickly and decisively to confront problem people.

I cannot overemphasize the importance of this. Remember, good teams are made up of people with options. If those other team members feel like you are going to leave bad apples in place, the good ones will leave to get a better environment. Now you have two problems instead of one problem, and the snowball is starting downhill.

In addition, the problem employee will inevitably begin to cause problems outside of your organization. Bad people are noticed and will create a negative impression of your organization and you.

I recently encountered this issue in one of our business partnerships. We had been having difficulty working through our partner's legal department to get contracts done and checks written. Worse, one of our partner's lawyers was sending off offensive emails that made me question whether to terminate the deal (which could be lucrative for us and our partner). After digging into everything, I found out that this company's legal department had caused them to lose other deals before our partner fixed the problem. It will be difficult to earn back the money that was lost and even harder for our partner to regain their industry reputation. The lesson is clear.

Close the Gap

1. How can a leader have the openness that encourages staff to say what they really think? Is this openness apparent in your organization? Why or why not?

_____

_____

_____

_____

_____

2. What are a pastor's dual roles? Are these roles well-balanced in your church? What pitfalls have played out in the past?

_____

_____

_____

_____

_____

3. Church and ministry staffers tend to be pre-motivated by the mission. How can presuming upon this pre-motivation be detrimental to staffers and the organization? How can you protect against this kind of pattern?

_____

_____

_____

_____

_____

4. Has your organization suffered from micromanagement? How can this culture be remedied and your team be empowered to execute?

_____

_____

_____

_____

_____

5. Do executives in your organization feel free to dis-
    agree when hammering out a plan or project? Are
    they able to maintain sound relationships when
    disagreements flare? If not, are they the right peo-
    ple for the job?

    _____

    _____

    _____

    _____

6. Is there room for improvement in your organi-
    zation's compensation structure? How can you
    retain the quality people you need *and* ensure a
    streamlined staff sufficient to accomplish the
    mission?

    _____

    _____

    _____

    _____

    _____

7. Are personnel and partnership issues being adequately addressed in your organization, or do you see evidence of "thumb-sucking"? What courses of action are needed? How can the need for healthy confrontation be more fully embraced in the future?

_____

_____

_____

_____

_____

Chapter 3

What No One Tells You

The organization is a reflection of its leader. This means that the pastor has to set the tone and by his actions (not his words) convey the organization's priorities.

As the leader of the church, the pastor needs to understand that the church and its activities are a reflection of its leader. This statement has two implications. First, over time the staff and lay leadership of the church will begin to reflect the values, attitudes, and priorities of their leader. This is a natural result of working and spending time with someone you respect—you want to please him or her, and as a result you begin to act in a way that will fulfill that goal.

An astute visitor to your church, either for business or spiritual reasons, can make some reasonable assumptions about the pastor based on how he or she is treated by the staff and volunteers. If punctuality is important to the pastor, that trait, over time, will become instilled in the staff and as a result become instilled in the lay leadership and volunteers. Not only will services begin on time and run on schedule, but everything else will be on time as well. Staff meetings will start on time, and people will get to work on time. If punctuality is not important to the pastor, then over time he or she will look around and wonder why every meeting, every service, and every event seems to start late.

———

Visitors can make reasonable assumptions about the pastor based on treatment by staff and volunteers.

———

It is a matter of priority. Whatever the issue is, if it is clearly a priority to the leader, it will also be a priority throughout the rest of the team. This is true for virtually anything, whether positive or negative. If customer service or treating people well is not a priority for the pastor, it will eventually cease to become a priority for everyone else.

The important point here is that words, to a large extent, do not matter. It is the leader's actions that matter. The leader can write countless memos and give speeches to the staff about the need for the organization to be focused on customer service, for example. However, until the leader's actions reflect that priority, it will not be reflected throughout the organization. The leader has to show his or her team how he or she wants people handled. He or she also has to guide the organization in a way that reflects the priority. You cannot say that customer service is the priority and then load your people with other responsibilities such that they have no time to focus on the customer. Priorities must be chosen carefully. At the end of the day, any organization can really only reflect a small handful of high-priority items. Choose well, and make it positive!

ARRANGING PRIORITIES

I have hit on this point before, but it is worth addressing again. One of the big issues for pastors is their innate creativity. By their very nature, most pastors are creative people. Their primary job is to tell stories—to tell make the gospel come alive for their congregants. The problem is that this creativity tends to spill over into every other area of the pastor's life, including church administration.

Here is a real life example of how this can negatively impact a ministry. I am friends with the leader of a large national ministry organization. This guy is truly brilliant, with a tremendous understanding of what makes people tick. He is also exceedingly creative. This guy doesn't have one good idea, he has ten— and that is the problem. Because this leader likes creativity, he inspires it in those around him. The result is that his organization is embarking on an endless parade of new projects. The reality, however, is that very few of the great ideas get the benefit of great execution. When it comes time to drill down into the details and actually accomplish something, the leader has mentally moved on. The end result is a tremendous amount of unrealized potential.

------·•·------

**Very few great ideas get the benefit
of great execution.**

------·•·------

As you can see, this is an issue of priority. This leader places a high value on being creative and coming up with the next great idea. At the same time, he doesn't place a priority on execution. Why? Because that is not what he does and not what he likes.

So, how can the problem be fixed? It's easy. First, the leader needs to bring in an executive (which he has done) who thrives on his weakness. He needs a number-two guy who enjoys and focuses on execution and getting projects from start to finish. Then, more importantly, he needs to continue to show that execution is priority through his actions. He needs to decide on one thing—one project, one initiative—and make sure that the entire organization is focused (including himself) on getting that project done and making it successful before starting anything else. When the leader begins to show self-control and reflect the value that execution is as important as the next great idea, so will his organization. However, he can easily undermine the effort by again shifting his focus to the next idea.

While setting and reflecting priorities in a positive way seems to be such a simple point, for most organizations it remains elusive. I think the reason is that priority-setting requires a leader to know and understand and embrace the very essence of him or herself and the organization he or she leads. As I said above, you can't have 50 priorities. You can have maybe two or three. This means that you need to have a solid handle on what you are all about. It is simple but important, and most people never get past the surface. They are for being successful or for growing their church, but they don't have a clear idea of, "These are the one or two things that set me apart from the crowd." Get a grasp on that simple concept; then you can set priorities that will work and be reflective of you.

Every leader needs a filter (based on organizational priorities) through which the brew of great ideas must pass.

The reality is that just because something is a great idea doesn't mean it is a great idea for you or your ministry. It may be a great idea for someone else but not for you. This is why every leader needs a filter. The leader needs to know very clearly what his or her organization is about, what it is trying to do, and what it needs to do to achieve that result. By having a firm grip on your organization's priorities and corporate essence, you will also have the filter you need to pass ideas through.

A good example from the business world is Southwest Airlines. Despite all of the problems and issues facing the airline industry—from 9/11 to fuel prices to union difficulties to a poor economy—Southwest has been consistently profitable in an industry covered in red ink. Why? One reason is that Southwest has a very clear idea of what it is. It is "the low cost air carrier." Every executive action that Southwest takes is designed to further that objective. Therefore, when someone has a new idea for how to make Southwest better, the first question is—will the idea help Southwest keep prices down? If the idea can help keep prices low, then it gets further evaluation. If not, it stops right there. Time and energy are not wasted on anything that cannot help further the central corporate goal—being the low-cost carrier.

Another similar example is the California burger chain In-N-Out Burger. My kids love this place and visit it when we are in LA. (I love it too but shouldn't eat it.) The menu is very simple—burgers, fries, shakes, and drinks—that is it. At a time when every other burger chain is offering everything from gourmet coffee to salads, In-N-Out keeps it simple. They have a formula that works for them, and the line is out the door. It may sound boring to just keep doing the same thing day after day, but it works.

It takes tremendous focus and discipline on the part of leadership to stick to a focus like In-N-Out or Southwest. That is why so few companies do it and why so few are as successful as an enterprise. It is easy to follow the crowd and try to be an innovator and the latest thing. But for the two companies I just mentioned, veering off the chosen path probably would have been disastrous.

This concept is equally applicable to your church or ministry. At a pastors' conference at The Potter's House in Dallas, I once heard Pastor Ed Young Jr. make a great point on this subject about his church, Fellowship Church in Grapevine. At Fellowship, the leadership has decided that the single most important thing is to create the best possible Sunday morning experience for its members and visitors. As a result, those activities in the church that receive the most attention are those that impact the Sunday morning experience. That experience starts in the parking lot and continues until the family gets in their car and leaves the parking lot.

Naturally, there are plenty of activities at Fellowship, but none get the attention like those items that impact Sunday morning.

Likewise, there are churches like The Dream Center in LA that focus on reaching the underserved community in which it is located. To reach this objective, The Dream Center creates a home for a multitude of different ministries (from Adopt-A-Block to food programs to street Sunday school) that help it reach that objective.

**You cannot say yes to everything
and be effective.**

You cannot say yes to everything and be effective. Therefore, the pastor has to set the priorities and set the tone. If the leader sets the priorities and his or her actions (more than his or her words) back up and reinforce the priorities, then over time the organization and staff will begin to reflect the priorities. In an organization with clear priorities, it will be those employees who best reflect that priority who should be rewarded. When the leader lives out the priority and rewards those who do as well, the snowball will have started downhill, and the organization will be well on the way to turning the priority

into a point of differentiation and a stepping stone for
success.

———————•◦•———————

**Pastors need to recognize that they live in a
largely insulated world and do in fact have
weaknesses.**

———————•◦•———————

GETTING OUTSIDE THE CHURCH

I commonly hear from pastors just how all-encompassing
and overwhelming a pastor's job can be. From preparing
for Sundays to mid-week Bible classes to counseling the
hurting to running an organization, it is all too easy for
the pastor's entire life and the lives of his or her family
members to become solely about the church.

While to a certain degree this comes with the job,
there are steps both a pastor and his or her family can
take to lessen the impact as well as potential impacts that
one needs to be aware of. First, in terms of lessening the
impact, I think that it is imperative that pastors and their
families develop interests outside of the church. Whether
it comes in the form of business interests, hobbies, community involvement, or some other activity, outside work
and interest can both help pastors and their families
remain grounded and see a bigger picture. It is a cliché,
but it is far too easy to find yourself in a place where you
can't see the forest for the trees. If you only talk to people
in your church and you only deal with church problems,

you can easily lose yourself and your perspective of the larger world.

In terms of the potential negative impact of living in a world insulated by the church, two issues arise. First, people choose to work at or attend a particular church largely because of an affinity they feel for the pastor. When most of the people anyone associates with on a daily basis all share an affinity and to some extent an idealized image of that person, it can serve to separate the pastor from a reality. If everyone around you thinks that you are great, that every sermon is great, that every decision is great, it can be difficult not to start "believing the press" so to speak. Outside relationships with people who "like you for you"—and not because of your position or what you do—are priceless.

———◆•◆•◆———

If everyone thinks everything you do is great, it can be difficult not to "believe the press."

———◆•◆•◆———

One of my favorite things that Bishop Jakes says is that we constantly need to be stretching ourselves. As he discussed in his book, *Reposition Yourself,* if you are consistently the smartest person in the room, you need to get into a different room. Said another way, get around people who stretch you, expand your mind, and view the world from a different perspective. You cannot grow as a person unless you surround yourself with people who have a knowledge and experience base that you lack.

Personally, one of my best professional decisions was to become involved with Parkland Hospital, the county-supported safety net hospital in Dallas. As part of my service, I spent several years on a blue ribbon committee that ultimately recommended and obtained voter approval for a $1.3 billion replacement hospital facility. The process was one of the most complex I had ever been involved with, both in terms of the politics and the sheer complexity of projecting Dallas' health care needs into the next half century. The rewards, however, were immense.

First, I got a bird's-eye view of how another organization tackled a difficult problem. Being a firsthand witness to such a long, complex process taught me lessons about how big issues can be broken down into manageable pieces for discussion and decision-making purposes. I also gained a unique understanding of how multiple groups with divergent interests can be brought together around a single big goal that ultimately would provide a positive result for everyone involved. The point is that new and different experiences in a world far removed from church and ministry can bring significant rewards.

Experiences in a world far removed from church and ministry can bring significant rewards.

At the same time, through my work on the blue ribbon committee, I also developed key relationships that have

benefited my daily life, both personally and profession-
ally. Because of the high-level contacts that I now have in
Dallas' medical community, I have been in a position to
provide some real help and assistance to people in need.
For example, I have a friend whose son recently suffered
a severe injury. Using my contacts, I was able to get my
friend the input and assistance that she needed to make
sure that her son was getting the help he needed.

On a professional level, my contacts with other members of the blue ribbon committee have led to positive
results in our business. For instance, my friendship with
one member of the committee who is also on the Texas
Arts Commission has helped both of us push forward a
mutual agenda to increase film and television work in the
Dallas area.

At the same time, hopefully I projected a positive
view of Bishop Jakes and his organization into the larger
Dallas community. It is a simple reality that most people
in your city don't know much about you or your organization. Even with an organization and leader like T.D.
Jakes, most people in Dallas have a very limited understanding of what we do. It is through outside involvement
in the community that people can learn, on a one-to-one
basis, what you do, who you are, and what you are about.
The point is that by developing meaningful relationships
outside of the church, not only will you protect yourself
from becoming a victim of living in an insulated world,
but you will also gain the benefit of expanding your
world, your mind, and your base of contacts. This is all
accomplished while also having an opportunity to show
others what you are all about. Not a bad deal. All it takes
(and I recognize that this is a big deal) is an investment of

your time and effort. I know your time is valuable, but an investment of yourself in the community will yield meaningful long-term rewards.

The second negative impact of living in an insulated world that is completely submersed in the church is that the pastor and his or her family may find themselves without an outlet for stress. Living in a world where you are constantly being called upon to deal with the problems of others can be very taxing and stressful. When your colleagues and friends are all a part of your church, it can leave you without anyone to turn to with your own issues, problems, and challenges. No matter what anyone in your congregation thinks, you are human. You do have problems and issues and we all need guidance, advice, or simply a sounding board from time to time.

You are human. You have problems and issues and need guidance or a sounding board from time to time.

As the pastor, you are in a way playing a role. In the course of my career, I have produced three stage productions, three movies (two more are in the works), and a sitcom, and I have learned a few things about playing a role. First, the lights are incredibly hot. Second, the camera shows every flaw. Third, playing a role is incredibly tiring. Just as it is difficult for an actor to stay in character, playing the role of pastor is equally taxing. Whereas the actor gets to change roles after the movie or go back to his trailer during set-ups, the pastor is always on stage. The lights are always on and the camera is rolling. This is exacerbated when the pastor's complete life is wrapped up in the church. Then, there is nowhere to relax, be yourself, and not have to worry about whether your makeup is right. The bottom line is that if you don't have a release, you will eventually melt under the heat of the lights.

To get the needed release, you and your family need meaningful outside relationships and outside interests. You need a piece of your life that isn't tied to church. At the same time, I strongly suggest that you find a refuge. Take vacations. You need to recharge your batteries on a regular basis, and you need to do so somewhere away from church and church people. If you are well known in your area, go somewhere where no one knows you. The point is that from time to time, you need to get off stage, get away from the lights, and relax!

In order to obtain success, the pastor needs to be empowered to follow the path that God sets for him or her.

Just as the staff needs to be empowered by the pastor to act, the pastor needs to be empowered by the congregation and board of directors. I am a firm believer that the pastor—not a committee or the board or the church membership—needs to have considerable latitude to act and needs to be protected in the corporate structure of the organization.

Whether a Fortune 500 corporation or a church, I do believe that the board of directors plays a vital role in terms of oversight, advice, guidance, support, and accountability. However, it is the CEO of the corporation, the pastor of the church, who needs to be empowered to set the direction and priorities of the organization.

This means the church's organizational documents and actual operating practice need to clearly establish roles and responsibilities. The pastor needs to understand what needs board approval and what does not. In the best circumstance, the pastor is using the board (like his staff) to fill the gaps of his expertise and to maximize his talents.

Ultimately, to make this work, the organizational documents (generally the bylaws and articles of incorporation) need to protect the pastor in his role. The documents, in my view, should make it very difficult for a board or church membership to remove a pastor for any reason other than the most serious offense.

The ousting of Larry Jones from Feed the Children or even Ted Haggard from his church should not have been such an easy thing for the board to do. I encourage you to take some time, look at your structure, and make sure that you understand it and that it works for you. There is a more in-depth discussion of this topic in the chapter on building a solid foundation.

———◆◆◆———

In a time of crisis, the leader needs to trust his or her instincts, do the right thing, and not be led astray by the so-called experts.

———◆◆◆———

I am a lawyer, and as such I value quality legal advice and counsel in a time of trouble. Likewise, public relations specialists can add significant value. And as we all know, there is wisdom in a multitude of counsel (see Prov. 11:14).

However, when the rubber hits the road and there is a real crisis to be dealt with—a decision on whether or not to make a statement or what the statement should say has to be made (do you respond to the interview request about some issue or hope it goes away?)—in those cases where the organization is potentially on the line, the leader needs to trust his or her instincts.

Yes, the leader needs to solicit counsel and advice from trusted advisors. Get the legal outlook (too often to do nothing in fear of doing the wrong thing); get the public relations outlook (too often to speak out without regard to the legal consequences); speak to those who have had a similar experience. Get all of the quality advice that you can get. But at the end of the day, you know your people and you know the right thing to do. Just do it.

Remember, in a crisis doing nothing is a decision and is almost always the wrong one.

**The leader must take care of him or herself
to be effective.**

LETTING GO

For a leader to make sound decisions, to properly motivate and inspire the staff, and to deliver his or her very best for the congregation each week, the leader must be properly rested, healthy, and in a great state of mind. This means that you need to take a few simple steps.

First, follow the advice of this book and recruit a great staff who can relieve you of many of the pressures of being a pastor. You need to be able to focus on the important matters and not have to worry about the less important but nonetheless time-consuming and worrisome tasks.

Next, take regular vacations. Go places where you are not known and you don't have to be "on" all of the time. Let your hair down and relax. If you have a good team in place, all will be well when you get back home.

Finally, and this can be difficult, as your church or ministry grows and the demands on your time grow along with the organization, you are going to have to leave some things behind. The pastor of a church of 250 people can shake every hand after service. The pastor of a church of 10,000 cannot. Likewise, you may need to restrict access to things like your cell number, your email, etc. Some of the people who had ready access to you when your church was in a living room may not be able to have access to you now. This "pulling back" can be painful for both the pastor and those who are pulled away from, but it is often necessary. You need a portion of your life that is just yours and your family's.

———————

You need a portion of your life that is just yours and your family's.

Bishop Jakes and I recently held a seminar for a small group of hand-selected pastors to talk about what it takes to get to the next level in ministry. This point about the need to let go of some things to give yourself the ability to reach others was a common refrain in our discussions. Just as running a large church requires different business skills than running a start-up church, a different set of interpersonal skills and relationships is also required. You have to pull back from certain duties and certain relationships. With a large congregation and added business responsibilities, you can't keep doing it all. You need to carefully pick and choose what you will do and will not do.

An important related point is that you need to be willing to let people leave. This one is truly difficult for a lot of pastors. No one wants to see members leave. However, as your church grows, you need to focus on where God is leading you and what is better for the church as a whole. You simply can't please everyone, and you shouldn't even try.

My wife and I were recently watching Joel Osteen and a Sunday morning. He gave a great sermon about how you can't be free until you stop worrying about what people think and focus instead on what God thinks. He told a story about how a certain church member kept telling him that he would leave the church if the location was changed, but Joel knew that moving the church to the Compaq Center was the right thing to do and what God wanted—the church needed the space. Joel had to tell the member to go ahead and leave because moving locations was best for the church. Now, any time he gets similar comments about leaving the church, he just tells them to leave. The result is a church run for God, and every time someone leaves another ten walk in the door.

The point is that you can't let a few negative people hold you back from your destiny. You have to grab what is in front of you, not hold onto the past.

CLOSE THE GAP

1. Priority-setting starts at the top. Are any "priority gaps" apparent in your organization? What is their origin, and how are they playing out organization-wide? What solutions will you offer?

   _____

   _____

   _____

   _____

2. How can you or your pastor/ leader's creativity be better harnessed to fulfill organization priorities?

   _____

   _____

   _____

   _____

3. How can the leader's knowledge of self and recognition of corporate essence be used to filter new ideas? Have these filters been working so far?

_____

_____

_____

_____

4. What are two common drawbacks of insulated
   leadership? How are you/your leaders addressing
   this concern?

_____

_____

_____

_____

5. Do your organizational documents and operating
   practices establish clear roles and responsibilities?
   How well do they protect the pastor/leader from
   being too easily ousted? What deficiencies exist,
   and how can they be addressed?

_____

_____

_____

_____

6. When the "rubber hits the road" in times of
   crisis, the leader must trust his or her instincts.
   Has this been the case in previous crises in your

organization? How might the next crisis be handled better?

_____

_____

_____

_____

7. In what specific areas has letting go proven difficult for you/your leader? What outcomes have resulted?

_____

_____

_____

_____

Chapter 4

Effectively Hiring and Managing Outside Professionals

In addition to your executive team, a critical element in the success of your overall organization will be the quality and the expertise of the outside professionals who become a de facto part of your organization. Here I am referring to the accountants, lawyers, consultants, public relations specialists, and other advisers who you will, by necessity, look to over time to help guide and counsel your organization as you navigate the treacherous waters of today's business world.

The first question you may be asking yourself is, "Why do I even need to worry about how to effectively hire and maintain a team of outside professionals?" The reason is fairly simple—today's legal and business climate has become incredibly complex and sophisticated. For example, while I consider myself to be an accomplished attorney and businessman, I frequently will engage the services of outside counsel, accountants, and other advisors to assist us in specific matters. The reason is that within certain areas of the law as well as in business, the world has become so complex and sophisticated that you simply need to be living in that world every day, on a day-in day-out basis, in order to keep up with the changes and shifts in the marketplace, the laws, etc.

Today's legal and business climate has become incredibly complex and sophisticated.

Additionally, talented professionals such as lawyers and public relations experts are generally very expensive and only need to be used on a limited or sporadic basis. As a result, most organizations cannot justify the cost of having such people on staff full-time. The alternative is to develop long-term relationships with quality advisors who can get to know your organization well and serve you over time.

While generally expensive on the front end, high-quality advisors over the long-term will easily save you far more than they cost you in terms of lost time, money, and aggravation. As your organization grows and prospers, it is unavoidable that by necessity you will need to hire, and as a result manage and oversee, the activities of lawyers, accountants, consultants, and other outside professionals. This experience like any other can prove to either be mutually rewarding or equally detrimental to both sides of the equation.

A great deal of success in these relationships depends on the approach you bring to the relationship. When working with professionals, try to remember a few basic rules. First, seek out and find the best person for your given situation. Most people treat lawyers, accountants, and other professionals like they are one size fits all. What I mean by this is that people believe that a good lawyer can handle any legal situation and that a good accountant is good to do the tax work for any business.

However, there is a significant difference between a criminal matter and a real estate deal, just as there is a difference between the accounting requirements of a church versus those of a Fortune 1000 company. Unfortunately, the problems encountered by organizations in this regard will not be aided by most professionals. Unfortunately, all too many professionals are interested in only getting paid and are hesitant to turn down anything they perceive to be a lucrative assignment. This is the case even if, in truth, they are not completely confident or prepared. And moreover, even fewer professionals are comfortable referring their clients to others who may try to steal the client and take over all of the client's work.

In this chapter, I will discuss the three primary advisors most organizations will need to avail themselves of—a lawyer, an accountant, and a public relations specialist.

WORKING WITH LAWYERS

In order to gain some understanding of what you need to look for in a lawyer, you need some background of how lawyers and the practice of law have developed over time. A hundred years ago, the practice of law was such that most lawyers practiced in individual offices and handled all their clients' various legal matters. One lawyer would handle any problem a client had. Whether that issue was creating a will, acquiring a piece of real estate, or handling a lawsuit, the one lawyer handled all of it. Today, the reality of lawyers—just like doctors, accountants, public relations experts, and business consultants—is much different. The law (like the world at large) is an ever-expanding, endlessly growing, complex set of rules. As a result, lawyers, like doctors and other professionals, have evolved into distinct levels of practice.

Lawyers, like doctors and other professionals, have evolved into distinct levels of practice.

One level is that of a traditional practice lawyer. This lawyer (comparable to your family physician) handles a wide variety of cases and matters and has a solid (but somewhat limited) knowledge of a multitude of practice areas. For example, the general practice lawyer may handle some lawsuits, some real estate matters, divorces, basic business transactions, estate matters, and some criminal cases. This lawyer takes on the cases his or her clients bring as long as he or she feels confident to handle the matter. In this way, the general practice lawyer is very much like your family physician. He or she can typically identify your problem, and in many cases, help you resolve the problem. At other times, he or she recognizes that he or she is out of his or her depth and that a specialist (who deals with your particular issue all of the time) is needed.

The weakness of the general practice lawyer is that he or she cannot know everything about everything and may not have a specific expertise that you need. Therefore, like your family doctor, a general practice lawyer can handle about 80 percent of what ails you. However, it is the other 20 percent you need to worry about.

A general practice lawyer can handle 80 percent of what ails you. You need to worry about the other 20 percent.

Because of the inability of the general practice lawyer to keep pace with the growing complexity of the law in every area of the law, the second tier of lawyers has developed. These lawyers focus their practice on a few narrow areas of the law in which they develop a high level of expertise, knowledge, and connections. Just as a cardiologist may devote his or her entire career to performing heart surgery, a lawyer may spend his or her entire career advising clients only on sophisticated tax matters. These lawyers, like medical specialists, are equipped to handle the most complex and unusual matters (within their area of expertise) that may arise in the course of your organization's work.

Specialist lawyers generally work in one of three settings. Most tend to work within large law firms that are made up of a large number of lawyers (sometimes hundreds) divided into diverse specialty areas of practice. As a result, you have a number of very large law firms (I started my legal career at one—they are great training grounds) made up entirely of specialists who effectively function as one-stop shops. Whether you need a highly qualified lawyer for a complex tax issue, a real estate matter, a corporate matter, or a dispute with a very significant amount of money at stake, most of the big firms will have someone who can handle your issue.

Outside of the big firms, specialists tend to work either alone or within small firms that are either smaller versions of the big firms (a group of lawyers with different but complimentary specialty areas) or small groups of lawyers with the same or related specialties (known as a boutique firm because they only do one or two areas). The specialty or "boutique" firms usually receive a lot of their business in the form of referrals from firms that do not have a lawyer with that particular specialty.

At first blush, larger law firms appear to be an ideal solution. You only need one law firm and every problem is handled by an expert in that specific area. However, the structure of these large law firms also creates a few disadvantages. First, the largest law firms tend to be much more expensive than smaller firms or a general practice lawyer. For example, partners in such firms typically charge anywhere from $400 to $900 per hour, plus expenses. Even associates, younger lawyers who don't yet own a portion of the firm but are instead employees, are prone to charge in the $200 to $500 per hour range, depending on their experience level. By comparison, even a senior partner in a general practice with 20 years of experience will probably only charge in the $250 to $450 range, depending on the city. There are a couple of reasons for the high cost of these firms. The lawyers are all specialists, the firms generally only recruit the top law students (and they pay them accordingly), and they have and use every possible resource and consequently have enormous overhead costs.

An additional disadvantage of some large law firms is that such firms will not even accept your organization as a client unless they expect you to give them a certain amount of work per year. For example, many major firms do not want clients who will not generate a minimum of $100,000 a year or more in annual billings. The reason is simple, as these firms primarily cater to America's corporate heavyweights who generate millions per year in legal work. It is simply viewed as unprofitable to allocate resources to a client who can only generate a limited amount of work.

In addition, because most of the lawyers in these firms are specialists, it is often difficult to get one lawyer in the firm with whom you can develop a long-term relationship. In my opinion, it is critical to have a good, solid relationship with at least one lawyer who can not only solve specific problems, but also acts as a general counselor or advisor to your organization. In order to act in that role, a lawyer needs to have a good overall understanding of your activities and organizational structure. It is difficult for a specialist who only works for you on sporadic matters limited to his or her area of expertise to accumulate that necessary institutional knowledge about your organization.

Find a lawyer who can solve specific problems *and* act as a general advisor to your organization.

Without the benefit of a lawyer with in-depth institutional knowledge of your organization, you will either spend inordinate amounts of time bringing different lawyers up to speed on your activities or you will have something critical missed. More than likely, you will have something missed. The reason is simple. If your organization is large, it is likely that multiple people in your organization will have contact with your outside lawyers. That contact will relate to their specific area of responsibility. However, the person in your organization dealing with your lawyer probably does not know everything about your organization. So if your representative does not have full knowledge or the lawyer does not have full knowledge, the advice that you get will be issue-specific but may not take into account some valuable piece of missed information.

For this reason, you need to be sure that you have at least one lawyer who is familiar with your organization and its activities and directives. In addition, you need to make sure that this lawyer is interfacing with a senior executive within your organization who similarly has full knowledge of the organization's activities and objectives. Therefore, the two people through which all the legal advice is funneled will have a full picture of your organization.

At the end of the day a lawyer with a wide and deep knowledge of your organization is likely to save you tens of thousands of dollars in legal fees. How is this possible? It's possible because lawyers usually charge by the hour. When a lawyer with a deep knowledge of your organization gives you advice in a ten-minute phone call that would have taken another lawyer five hours (because that lawyer would have to ask questions and gather information), you have saved at least $1,000.

A lawyer with a wide and deep knowledge of your organization can save tens of thousands in legal fees.

Therefore, my suggestion is to be aware of and utilize a multitude of counsel. Both law firm models discussed above have rightful places. At the outset, your organization needs a good general practice lawyer. He or she will act as your family physician, treating the occasional illness and hopefully dispensing quality advice on healthy living. While they are relatively rare, it is wise to seek out a lawyer who has some experience and expertise representing ministries, churches, and other nonprofit organizations.

Choosing a Lawyer

If you cannot find a suitable lawyer with experience representing churches or other ministries, remember that your church or ministry is a nonprofit corporation just like the United Way, the Boy Scouts, a university, or most hospitals. Therefore, a lawyer who has experience in other types of nonprofits will likely understand the core issues faced by your organization even though he or she might not have notable experience in a church or ministry specifically.

Then, as your organization grows and prospers, your needs will become increasingly complex. As your needs change, you will need to expand your legal base to include specialists in different areas. For example, all large churches have one thing in common—the need for a large meeting place or sanctuary. To find an existing small church building or building a $3 million facility is one thing. But planning the construction of a $50 million or a $100 million facility is something entirely different. It would be the rare general practice lawyer who is qualified to negotiate a $100 million construction contract with a major contractor and simultaneously negotiate and close a $75 million credit facility with a major bank. In that scenario, you would be advised to have someone with extensive experience working on such complex real estate and financial matters.

Similarly, if your church decides to engage in any activity in the entertainment business, whether it is simply as an artist with a record company, a first-time book publishing deal, or something as complex as forming a record label and producing music, you will need to obtain specialized advice. The entertainment business, both in the Christian and secular marketplaces, is one of the most shark-infested realms you could ever dive into. Entertainment companies have been taking advantage of amateurs for all of history. If you do not arm yourself, you are likely to become someone's lunch in that world.

The problem with this dual prong strategy when using lawyers is knowing when to get specialized help. Hopefully, you've chosen a wise and competent lawyer who is going to lead you to get specialized help when you need it. If not, the burden will be on you to know when to seek outside help. In order to know when you've reached that point, you need to know your regular lawyer. Over time, you should obtain a sense of his or her character. In addition, you should also obtain a sense for what he or she is good at. Just as with your employees, it is critical to become comfortable with the skills and limitations of your lawyers and other professional advisors. Don't be afraid to continually evaluate your professional advisors and lawyers and continually assess their qualifications. Ask questions. Has he or she ever done this particular type of work before? Make the person be specific. Have the lawyer tell you about the case and the amounts of money involved, and ask to talk to the other clients.

The process of learning your lawyer begins at the outset of the relationship. You should interview potential lawyers as if you were hiring them to be another employee. I cannot tell you how many times a new client who I did not know and who did not know me simply dropped a very important matter into my lap and followed my advice without ever finding out what I could really do. Hopefully I lived up to the expectations of those trusting clients. However, I was always struck by how much faith those people placed in me solely on the basis of my reputation or referral from another client.

While lawyers and other professionals don't encourage it, you should feel free to interview prospective lawyers and ask very difficult questions. In addition, talk to other clients of the lawyer. Both good and bad reputations spread quickly, and it is usually easy to track down a lawyer's reputation in your area. If a prospective lawyer gives the impression that he or she does not have time or is offended by the process, you are talking to the wrong person. I can assure you that when lawyers go looking for counsel to handle a particular matter for them, they interview and go through the steps I have just suggested.

If a prospective lawyer is offended by the interview process, you are talking to the wrong person.

In the course of the interview, explain your organization, its size and challenges, and get the lawyer to explain their relevant expertise. Find out where the lawyer went to school. How well did the lawyer do in school? While the quality of the lawyer's legal education is, of course, not completely indicative of the lawyer, it can be helpful. For example, most large law firms rarely hire lawyers who don't graduate in the top 10 to 15 percent of their class. Success in law school typically will equate to a lawyer with very good technical understanding of the law. As a result, most highly successful law students gravitate toward careers as specialists.

If you need a specialist, such as a tax lawyer, I would tend to stay away from lawyers with less than stellar academic backgrounds.

On the other hand, if you need a trial lawyer because you've been sued or criminal allegations have been made against you, then you need a lawyer who is part performer and part gunfighter. A trial involves the telling of a story in an adversarial setting. Therefore, you need to find someone who will take up your cause and fight for you. Several of the best trial lawyers barely made it through law school, but they know how to fight. Remember, a lawsuit is a street fight played out by actors, and you need to hire accordingly.

You should keep a few important quotes in mind as you make your final decisions in hiring an attorney. First, one very important question is who will be your point of contact in the law firm and who will do most of your work. You need to make sure that you meet both of the lawyers—the lawyer who is your point of contact and the lawyer who will do most of the work for you. Most successful firms have one or more "rainmakers" who are primarily responsible for bringing in new business. These "rainmakers" are often very expensive, very experienced, very smooth, and very impressive salesmen who rarely do any of the real legal work. Their task is to solely generate new client relationships and manage and maintain those relationships. Therefore, when the work comes into the office, it is typically delegated to a younger, less-experienced lawyer. The moral is to be careful if you've selected a firm solely because you were impressed by the senior partner. The key is to be impressed by both the lawyer who gets the work and the lawyer who does the work.

A second related point is the accessibility of the lawyers that you choose. By definition, most good lawyers are in demand and are very busy people. However, your lawyer cannot do you any good if you do not have ready access to him or her and cannot get timely responses. Therefore, while you want a lawyer who is in demand, you also want a lawyer who is wise enough to limit his or her practice enough to allow him or her to responsibly service all his or her clients.

Pay attention to the small signs. How long does it take your lawyer to return your phone call?

For obvious reasons, the extent to which your lawyer is overburdened is difficult to judge prior to your becoming a client. It will likely take time to see exactly how available he or she is to you. Most lawyers tend to make an extra effort with new clients, so it may take until the "honeymoon" period is over to determine how your lawyer will do. However, pay attention to the small signs. How long does it take the lawyer to return your phone call? It should be 24 hours or less. Does every communication with your lawyer get filtered through a paralegal or a secretary? I would suggest you start looking for a new lawyer if you know his or her assistant better than you know the lawyer. Lawyers who are too busy to adequately service their clients frequently push too much work onto their assistants and paralegals. The only communication that you should be having with your lawyer's assistant should be concerning logistical and informational matters. The assistant should be the one setting up the conference call or asking for a copy of a document or answering a simple factual question such as has a certain act been completed, etc. What should not be accepted is a back-and-forth dialogue with the assistant where you have to ask the assistant your question and then wait for the assistant to ask the lawyer and call you back. There is simply too much potential to lose valuable information in the translation, and a lawyer who relies too heavily on such a process should probably not be trusted to correctly convey advice.

A good lawyer needs to know the big picture of your organization.

Once you've identified a quality lawyer with whom you have a rapport, develop a relationship. Involve that lawyer in your affairs to the extent that you can. It is very difficult to counsel a client in a vacuum. A good lawyer needs to know the big picture of your organization in order to fully and properly understand how a specific matter may affect other areas of the organization.

BILLING

The next major issue involving the management of lawyers is that of cost. For the most part, lawyers bill in three ways. The most basic and common form of billing is a straight hourly fee. In this scenario, the lawyer bills the client for the actual amount of time he or she spends working on the matter. The time spent is multiplied by the lawyer's hourly rate to determine the bill.

The next method is percentage fees. Typically used by the plaintiff's lawyers representing the victim in an injury case, this involves the lawyer billing for a percentage of the amount he or she wins for you in the case. Percentage billing is sometimes also used by several lawyers in the entertainment business who will bill clients for a percentage of the deal obtained. Often in this circumstance the lawyer is acting more like an agent or a manager in addition to providing pure legal work.

The third way lawyers bill their clients is flat rate billing. In this scenario a lawyer bills a client a set amount to complete a specified task. For instance, you and your lawyer may agree that he or she will handle a real estate deal from start to finish in exchange for a flat fee of $25,000. In a related format, some lawyers charge you monthly retainers that entitle you to certain legal services during that calendar month.

The arrangement that you and your lawyer should settle on depends on the circumstances and negotiations. Generally the fairest is straight hourly billing as the lawyer gets paid for the time he or she actually spends working for you and that's all that you pay for.

With percentage billing, the lawyer typically ends up with a much higher hourly fee if he or she is successful. This may or may not represent a good deal for you, the client. For instance, you may be looking for a book deal. A good lawyer/book agent may charge you 10 percent to

15 percent of the value of the deal that he or she gets for you. In that circumstance, the lawyer is not only responsible for getting the deal but also explaining the legal work related to the deal.

As an example, that lawyer may spend 20 hours getting you the deal and doing the related legal work for a book deal that paid you a $100,000 advance, and the lawyer earns $15,000 or $750 per hour. That may be a good deal in the circumstance where you were buying the lawyer's contacts and knowledge as well as their legal expertise. In effect, you were paying the lawyer for two services, first to get you the deal and second to negotiate the deal. However, if you'd gotten the deal on your own and only needed the lawyer to do the legal work, then you probably would have overpaid for the purely legal aspects of the services that he or she provided.

The good and bad of these percentage deals is that you become partners with your lawyer. As a case is close to settling or a deal is close to being closed, you and your lawyer may form different opinions, depending on how risk averse each party is and what their objectives are. For example, you need to understand that a lawyer working on a percentage is likely to push for completion of a deal so that he or she can get paid, even if that deal may not be the best ultimate result for you.

———————

**A lawyer working on a percentage is likely
to push for completion of a deal so that he
or she can get paid.**

———————

Regardless of the billing arrangement, remember this—the client, that is you, should always make the decisions. Your lawyer cannot settle a case or agree to contract terms without your consent. If your lawyer has tried to say that he or she has such rights or put such rights into your attorney/client contract, get a new lawyer and call the local bar association. The lawyer simply cannot substitute his or her view for that of the client. To do so is improper and unethical.

MANAGING YOUR LAWYER

Once you have found a qualified lawyer and entered into an agreement that specifies how your lawyer will be paid, it is time to develp a better relationship with and manage your lawyer. This is the point where most clients run into trouble. Too often, clients will put up with subpar service, lack of accessibility, sloppy billing practices, and a lack of accountability. Remember, you are paying first-class prices, and you are entitled to first-class service. If you do not get it, move on. Your legal and professional matters are far too important to settle for mediocre representation.

You are paying first-class prices and are entitled to first-class service.

With that in mind, here's my version of a client's bill of rights. Having been both a practicing lawyer and a consumer of legal services from some of the best in the business, I'm uniquely qualified for this subject.

A CLIENT'S BILL OF RIGHTS

1. The client shall set the objectives of the representation and make all business decisions involved in the representation.

2. The client is entitled to a full discussion and explanation of any legal strategy proposed by his or her lawyer.

3. The client is entitled to prompt response of representation. All client phone calls should be returned promptly.

4. The client is entitled to regular progress reports on all pending matters.

5. The client is entitled to an honest assessment on the time required to complete a task and adherence to reasonable deadlines.

6. The client is entitled to clear, accurate, and detailed billing.

7. The client is entitled to complete confidentiality of all information learned by the lawyer during representation.

8. The client is entitled to full disclosure from the lawyer of all settlement offers and contract proposals.

9. The client is entitled to full disclosure of any potential conflicts of interests the lawyer may have.

10. The client is entitled to integrity and honesty from the lawyer.

If your lawyer complies to this bill of rights, you have found good, honest, responsive legal representation.

While the foregoing points have been specifically addressed to the attorney/client relationship, they are equally applicable to relationships with accountants, consultants, bankers, and other professionals. These professionals can and should be valuable members of your executive team and should, at the end of the day, be good investments both in terms of the money spent and the effort put forward by you to develop and to build the relationship. At the end of the day, competent professionals should add value to your organization, make your executive team better employees, and give you confidence to know your organization is being well managed.

------◆·◆·◆------

At the end of the day, competent professionals should add value to your organization.

------◆·◆·◆------

WORKING WITH ACCOUNTANTS

Most of the above discussion regarding lawyers is applicable to accountants. Accountants tend to organize themselves in basically the same manner as lawyers. There are a few mega-firms (the accounting equivalent of the large national law firms) that are made up of specialists from many different specialties. Then you have the smaller boutique firms and the general practice firms and solo practices.

Just as with the general practice lawyer, the general practice accountant should be able to take care of most of your needs. The more specialized and complex work needs someone dedicated to that specific area of accounting.

However, there are a couple of unique issues that need to be addressed. First, the economic lifeblood of any church or nonprofit is its tax-exempt status. Without the tax exemption, you cannot accept tax-deductible donations. Clearly, you cannot be too careful with your exempt status.

Accordingly, I strongly advise every church and ministry to use an accountant with meaningful experience representing nonprofit organizations. You need someone who not only knows general accounting but also the special tax rules related to nonprofits.

You need an accountant who knows general accounting and the special tax rules related to nonprofits.

Next, you need to understand that you need accountants for two primary reasons. First, you need to make sure that the transactions that your organization engages in are properly documented and accounted for—the basic finance stuff that every business has to deal with—making sure that the assets, liabilities, income, and expenses of the organization are recorded properly so that you have a clear understanding of your financial health.

Next, you want the accountants to conduct audits of your finances. The objective of the audit is to ensure that your processes, systems, and procedures are adequate and sufficiently protect the organization. During the audit, the accountants will spot check your records to determine if errors and weaknesses are present and whether your organization's financial statements are an accurate reflection of reality.

The audit gives you two basic benefits. One is that it shows outsiders (like lenders) that your financials can be relied upon. The audit also shows you (and indirectly, third parties) that your systems are adequate. If the systems have weaknesses or if your in-house people are making mistakes, the audit should reveal the problems. Then, the audit firm should use the information to help coach and guide your in-house team so that the same mistakes are not made and so that processes and systems are made better.

One important note here on audit fees. While fees will naturally go up as the size and complexity of your organization increases, fees should actually go down over time (if your organization is not growing significantly) because the audit firm should be making your staff better each year. As your team gets better, there should be less for the auditors to deal with, and consequently, fees should go down. If the fees are always on the rise and your organization is not growing in a big way, you have a problem with your audit firm.

One other note on auditors. You do not want to frequently change firms. Doing so generally creates an impression that you are attempting to hide improper accounting practices. In addition, frequently changing firms will generally result in increased fees because each audit requires both the audit firm and your staff to go through a learning curve.

Last, the audit firm should be focused on matters of significance. All too often, I have seen audit firms spend excessive amounts of time and money chasing insignificant amounts of money. While it is technically true that even a very small dollar amount, improperly handled, could theoretically result in a problem in the event of an IRS audit, the reality is that doesn't happen. Accordingly, audit firms who focus on such minor issues are just driving up fees, not providing a valued service.

WORKING WITH PUBLIC RELATIONS SPECIALISTS

Just as with accountants, most of the logic set forth above with respect to lawyers applies to PR firms. They are also organized in a similar fashion and are made up of generalists and specialists.

However, instead of knowledge of a specific area of law or tax issues, PR firms tend to specialize in certain types of media relationships and certain types of advice. With PR firms, it all really comes down to the relationships with individual media outlets that the firm or individual has as well as the types of issues that they are accustomed to dealing with that matter.

One firm is great with entertainment issues and another is great with crisis management. Similarly, one firm may have great contacts with African American newspapers while another has great relationships at the big national newspapers. Who you need depends on who you are trying to reach.

One of the big questions that I get is, "How do you hold a PR firm accountable?" What they do appears, in the best of circumstances, to be a murky business with little in the way of measurable results. At our organization, we ask PR firms to provide us with details on all of the media exposure for our organization they have obtained. In turn, each piece of media can be valued. PR (which by definition is free media) is valued by looking at the cost to buy an equal amount of exposure through paid advertising. If what you are paying for PR expertise outweighs the value of the exposure obtained, you need new PR people.

If your PR costs outweigh the value of the exposure obtained, you need new PR people.

In addition to obtaining free media for you, PR should also play the roles of counselor, advisor, and teacher. They should teach you, if need be, how to be a good interview, how to get your point across, and how to avoid common pitfalls. Likewise, they should prepare you and make sure that you have the information needed to properly respond during the interview.

More importantly, the PR firm should be acting as a filter and advising which interviews are beneficial and which are not. As my constant refrain goes, you cannot do everything. Not all press and not all interviews are worthwhile. You need to know the interviewer, the outlet, what the rules are, and whether the end result is likely to be positive or negative.

At the end of the day, you need to find and develop a relationship with a group of outside professionals who can help you fill in the gaps on your leadership team. Lawyers, accountants, and public relations experts are the most common experts used by religious organizations. When you have the right ones, you and your organization will benefit tremendously from the added expertise. These folks will be expensive, but if you have the right ones, they will more than pay for themselves in exposure obtained, money saved, and avoided problems.

Moreover, the principles set forth here with regard to lawyers, accountants, and PR specialists can be equally applied to other specialty areas that your organization may need from time to time. Always go for quality, and find experts who get what you are trying to do and can add value outside of their core service.

You have built a great team of executives and outside experts to help fulfill and execute the mission of your organization. Now it is time to focus on the objective and get things done!

CLOSE THE GAP

1. Has your organization retained the services of professional advisors? If so, what specific benefits have resulted from their expertise? If not, were your outcomes satisfactory? Explain.

   _____

   _____

   _____

   _____

2. Do you have an attorney? If so, does he or she
    have in-depth knowledge of your organization? If
    not, how do you plan to find an attorney or get
    your current attorney up to speed?

    _____

    _____

    _____

    _____

3. When seeking counsel, have you taken the time to
    interview attorneys and their clients? If not, how
    did you decide who you would retain?

    _____

    _____

    _____

    _____

4. Have you received inferior service from an attor-
    ney or other professional? Where did he or she fail
    you? Did you hold the professional to account or
    tolerate the poor service? Explain.

    _____

    _____

    _____

    _____

5. What are the two primary services your accountant provides? If you are a church, ministry, or other non-profit organization, have you retained an accountant with nonprofit expertise? Why or why not?

    _____

    _____

    _____

    _____

6. Does your accountant drive up costs by "majoring in minors"? Do you track activity well enough to know? How can you do a better job assessing fees and activity in the future?

    _____

    _____

    _____

    _____

7. Does your organization regularly require PR services? If so, have you retained the right firm to suit the need? If your organization does not use PR services, how would such services add value?

    _____

    _____

    _____

    _____

Section 2

Speaking to the Staff

WHAT TO KNOW BEFORE YOU APPLY

Working as a senior executive in the world of ministry and faith-related business can be both challenging and incredibly rewarding. Over the course of my years advising and running ministry-related organizations, I have seen a lot of talented people who didn't fit within this environment, and other people have thrived. So what separates those who thrive from those who don't? A few characteristics stand out.

First, and most important, just as becoming a minister is a calling, so is working in a key leadership position in a church or ministry. If this is not where God wants you and if you don't have a passion for what you are doing, it is not going to work. There are plenty of ways to make money without the added stress and responsibility that come with ministry work. So before you go down this path, make sure that you are clear on your motivations and why you want to go down this path. If God is not in it, no amount of desire can make it work.

Next, you need to be able to separate ministry and business. You may work in a ministry, but at the end of the day, you are there to work, reach your goals, and achieve a positive result. A career in ministry does not equate to a career of going to church every day.

————◆————

**A career in ministry does not equate to a
career of going to church every day.**

————◆————

I think a lot of people (and churches) get into problems in the following circumstance. Joe belongs to his local church; he may or may not be happy in his current career, but he feels passionate and excited about his church and his pastor. Joe starts doing volunteer work for the church, and that is great. Then, one day, the church has an open position in Joe's field. Joe applies and gets the job. Then, after a while, Joe leaves the job and the church feeling disillusioned. Why?

One reason is that many underestimate the complexity of working in a large religious organization. They confuse the level of expectation placed on volunteers with the level of expectation placed on employees. After all, going to church and being a volunteer is easy; working at the church can't be much different. Then reality sets in. This is real work. In many respects, it is more challenging than working in the traditional business world. In the church world, you typically have fewer resources to work with, not as much support, and have to be creative to get things done.

Additionally, some take the position for the wrong reason. Just because a door opens doesn't mean that God wants you to walk through it. Take the time to listen to God and be sure that the move is what He intended.

Those who succeed in ministry work also understand the multiple levels of accountability for which they are responsible. As with any employee, you are accountable to your boss—the pastor or some other leader in the ministry. In this world, however, you also have a responsibility to the ministry, the congregation (if it is a church), and God. If you think about it, that is a lot of responsibility.

You cannot take this position lightly and hope to have success.

Because of this heightened level of responsibility, it is imperative that you have the ability to both defer to and follow the lead of the pastor, but also be a truth teller who will make sure (in an appropriate fashion and at an appropriate time) that the leader knows if you have well-founded misgivings about a course of action.

CLOSE THE GAP

1. Do you have any ministry staffers whose calling is uncertain? How do their actions or performance reveal this?

   _____

   _____

   _____

   _____

2. What does it mean to separate ministry and business? Are you doing this successfully? If you have staffers who report to you, are they doing this successfully?

   _____

   _____

   _____

   _____

3. How have the multiple levels of accountability in ministry been handled by your team overall? What coaching might be needed?

_____

_____

_____

_____

Chapter 5

Managing Up

One of the unique aspects of this book is that it is written from the perspective of someone who is not the top leader of the organization I work in. I am in the number two position. That means over my career I have had to both manage down (what most people think of in managing a staff that reports to me) but also manage up.

What do I mean by "managing up"? Managing up is the process of managing your relationship with your boss or bosses, as the case may be. Whether we recognize it or not, we are all engaged in the process of managing up. For the vast majority of us who are employed, the relationship is pretty clear. We have a boss who we report to every day. The process of managing your relationship with your boss is managing up.

Even the CEO of a Fortune 500 company has to manage up. While the CEO doesn't have a boss per se, he or she is accountable to both the board of directors and the shareholders of the company. If the CEO doesn't manage up and work those relationships well, he or she will not be the CEO long.

Even those who own their own business have to manage up to some extent. If you use financing in your business, you need to manage the relationship with your lender. The customers who determine whether you have revenue have to be managed.

So regardless of whether you work in a religious organization or not, managing up is a valuable skill set that needs to be mastered in order to have real success. The first step is understanding that managing up requires a skill set that is markedly different from the process of managing down.

Managing up requires a skill set that is markedly different from that of managing down.

Unlike the person who is managing down, the person who is managing up cannot take advantage of position or "granted authority" to motivate his or her superior. There is no "because I said so." Instead, managing up is based upon the ability to gain influence and work in a mutually beneficial manner with someone who, at the end of the day, can choose whether or not to work with you.

To me, the foundation of managing up can be summed up in a single word: trust. The process of effectively managing up is simply the process of building and maintaining trust in the relationship you have with your boss. As your boss comes to learn and understand that you are worthy of trust and that you have his or her back, then you are truly valuable—and nearly indispensible. Employees are easy to replace; an employee who is a trusted partner in business or ministry is something else entirely. Remember, your job is largely to free the leader to focus on other issues. To be able to do that, the leader has to be confident that you will perform. He has to trust you.

So how do you build trust in an employment situation? As with any other relationship in your life, building trust requires time, patience, and letting your actions speak far louder than your words.

BUILDING TRUST

The first element in building trust is to simply do what you say you are going to do. When you say that you will finish a project in two weeks, finish it in two weeks. If you cannot finish it in two weeks, make sure that there is a good reason and that you clearly communicate the issue, the problems, and what you are doing to resolve the problems and when you will get it done. You know if you will not be able to reach a deadline or not. Be up front and explain—before the project is late. The biggest mistake is to try to explain after you have been called on being late.

Always avoid over-promising.

A related point is that you should always avoid over-promising. I have seen it time after time. In an effort to impress, a new and promising employee lets his mouth write checks he can't cash. In the heat of the meeting, the employee starts talking about how he can do this or do that. If you really can, that is fine. But if you don't *know* that you can, it is just false bravado, and it will inevitably bite you. There are two bad consequences to over-promising, especially in an open meeting with your boss and your co-workers. First, most people who over-promise do so in a vain attempt to look good in front of the boss, usually at the expense of someone else. This means that your co-workers (people who you need to work with you) may feel as though you were trying to one-up them in front of the boss. Second, whether he or she says anything or not, your boss will notice when the promises come up empty.

Now you will have started yourself down a path that can be a very slippery slope. You have made one promise that didn't come to fruition. Now, it is all too easy to make another over-promise in an effort to make up for the failure. At the same time, you may have lost valuable allies in the trenches. The pattern does not have to continue for very long until everyone—your boss, your subordinates (if you have them), and your equals—will quickly learn that they shouldn't give too much credence to what you say. That means your co-workers are going to be reluctant to back and support you. No one wants to tie themselves to someone who may be on the way out the door. The bottom line is that you very quickly get into a situation where no one trusts you. As a result, you have no influence and no value.

While you don't want to over-promise, you also should not hold back. When you know something, say so. Another element in building trust is to exhibit the quiet confidence that says you are competent, you know your job, and you will perform. This confidence comes from being knowledgeable and comfortable with your area and subject matter. This means you need to keep up. You always need to be learning. Read the relevant trade magazines and websites. Get to know other people in your area. Becoming a constant, consistent learner will give you confidence in what you are doing. You will be surprised how it will show.

If you are the smartest person in the room, you are in the wrong room. You need to constantly stretch.

One of the great things that Bishop Jakes has instilled in me is that you if you are the smartest person in the room, you are in the wrong room. You need to constantly stretch and push yourself. Spend time around people who know more than you or have more experience that you do about certain subjects. Ask questions. Dig and get information.

For me, this is where I get a great deal of satisfaction. In running TDJ Enterprises, I work across a variety of industries. I am involved in businesses ranging from film and television to publishing to music to online businesses to real estate and investments. As a result, I am constantly around people who are among the best in their respective fields. By being exposed to these talented people on an ongoing basis, I am stretched and pulled and grow as a result. With each project, my base of knowledge and contacts grow. As my knowledge grows, so does my confidence in my own abilities. I know what I can do, what I might be able to do, and what the difference is.

It is all about finding balance and having a well-honed internal sense of your strengths and weaknesses. When you are confident, you can instill confidence in others (your boss, co-workers, and subordinates). As others gain confidence in you, the trust factor will grow, and your ability to influence others will increase as a result.

A closely related point on the issue of doing what you say is to make sure that you clearly understand what it is that you are being asked to do. If you don't, ask questions and get clarity. Don't waste valuable time and effort pursuing a path that you don't know to be the right one. Bishop Jakes ends virtually every meeting the same—with the question, "Are all hearts and minds clear?" Why? Because if you are not clear on something, the meeting needs to continue until you are.

Remember, as a senior executive supporting a pastor or ministry leader, you have two primary responsibilities—to free the leader to focus on critical matters and to make the vision of the leader a reality.

LINES OF AUTHORITY

The critical dynamic that needs to be worked out between the ministry leader and his top executives is the lines of responsibility and authority. As we have discussed before, in order for your team to reach maximum effectiveness, the team needs to be empowered. At the same time, the leader has an obligation to make sure that he or she is aware of what is happening and approves of it. This is where the tension is. There is no easy answer here. In my view, it is an evolving relationship. Over time, as long as there is a solid foundation of mutual respect from the outset, a comfortable working relationship will develop. As people become more accustomed to working with others and more aware of each other's strengths, weaknesses, and points of sensitivity, the authority levels will generally work themselves out.

For objective matters, like the authority to approve contracts or expenditures, there should be clearly defined limits. "You can approve up to this amount, and above that you need some other level of authority to sign off." Those are the easy issues.

The more difficult issues revolve around the subjective part of business. These are the decisions that involve the vision, direction, or approach of the organization or require a level of taste or preference or discretion. If you know your organization and your superior well and you have a clear understanding of what you are trying to achieve, these discretionary matters become easier. However, it is usually a longer process for people to get comfortable with someone else making subjective decisions for them.

---•◦•---

**Making sure your boss knows *why* is as important
as your boss knowing *what* you are doing.**

---•◦•---

From the standpoint of the executive who reports to
the ministry leader, a big part of this process (and your
job) is to keep the leader informed. Regular updates
(whether in person, by phone, or by email) are critical.
You don't want the leader wondering what you are doing
or why. Remember, making sure that your boss knows
"why" you want to do something is as important as your
boss knowing "what" you are doing. By clearly conveying
your reasoning and your thought process, you will not
only give credence to your decision (if you can't clearly
explain a decision, you shouldn't have made it) but you
will give your boss a valuable insight into how you think
and analyze problems. Over time you will find that your
influence with your boss will increase even when he disagrees with you because he has developed faith in your
thought process. He knows that your viewpoint was the
result of a thoughtful process and that it is worthy of
attention and consideration. As you follow these steps,
the trust factor will quickly grow.

From the standpoint of the leader, it is amazing what
you can learn from simply walking around your building,
talking to people, or making calls to your key people—
you should always be asking questions. If your people
know that they may get a call at any time about any topic
in their portfolio of responsibility, they will make an

effort to be sure they have the answers (or can get them quickly).

No one likes to be micro-managed. We all want a level of freedom and discretion in how we go about our daily work. This is absolutely true of the type of people you want helping to run your organization—great executives are by definition smart, ambitious people who relish a challenge. This means that managing high-quality executives requires a more subtle touch than managing people who are performing a more basic function.

Even though you have "authority," you need to manage by relationship and influence. A great way to do this is to simply spend time with your team engaged in dialogue. Talk about the things that are important to you. Ask a lot of questions. Delve into the "why." In this way, your process will actually aid in the process of developing respect and trust. The leader's questions will bring out the executive's thought process even if the executive isn't accustomed to sharing his or her thoughts.

Remember, just as a primary goal of your leadership team is to free the leader to focus on the big issues, the leader needs to actively work to make his team better.

———————

As an executive, your job is to solve problems, not merely pass them along.

———————

As that level of trust grows, you need to continue to expand your value by being a problem-solver, not a problem-passer. Obviously, there are major issues that require the top leader to weigh in and ultimately make a decision. However, even in those cases your job as a senior executive is to 1) know whether the issue really is important or not, 2) have thoroughly looked at the problem and developed the possible solutions, and 3) present the problem and possible answers to your boss. If you have done that, you have done all that can be asked.

On the other hand, if you encounter a problem and merely give it to your boss and say, "What do you want to do?" what good are you? Your boss can get to that point with or without you. You need to add value to every situation. You don't have to always be right; you just have to try to be right all the time. Do your homework, ask questions of your team, talk to other organizations, etc. Gather information and present your boss with options and reasons for each. By doing your homework, you will have fulfilled a vital role—you added value and freed your boss to focus on the issue and not to have to spend his time looking for answers.

My wife, Julaina, is a very successful businessperson and a great manager of people. One of the constant refrains that both our children and her staff hear is to be a problem solver. Whether it is our five-year-old daughter or a subordinate at work, there is no faster way to get on Julaina's bad list than to simply bring her a problem that could have and should have easily been solved without her. I am so happy that Julaina is actively working to instill in our children that they need to be problem-solvers. It is a quality that will serve them throughout life, no matter what they do. Weak people who cannot add value to a process simply are not valuable.

Another valuable element of managing up is to manage the expectations of the boss. When your boss comes to you with a plan, it is your job to dig in, do your homework, and come back to him and let him know: 1) how long will it take, 2) what resources you need (in terms of people and money), 3) what the potential problems are (and how you plan to overcome them), and 4) what you need from him.

If the boss' plan has problems, it is up to you to let him know what the issues are and what potentially can be done to help solve the problem. Likewise, you need to make sure that everyone is realistic about what is required to achieve a particular goal. For example, it may be perfectly feasible to get something done within the time frame that we originally requested, but your boss needs to know if in the process of getting the task done you will also have to use up every other resource available to the organization and as a result five other things will not get done.

Just as the boss needs to be clear with you about what he expects, you need to be clear with the boss about what his expectations will require. The boss may really want to take a particular course of action, but when he has all of the information and knows the real costs (not just in money but also in terms of time, effort, and other resources), he may or may not feel the goal is worth the cost.

———•·•·•———

The boss needs to be clear about what he or she expects; you need to be clear about what it will require.

———•·•·•———

The critical element in any decision-making process is reliance on good information. That is where the executive staff plays a critical role. You have to make sure that both you and the boss have all of the needed information and that the information is solid. Once you have done your homework and have good information, then the information can be analyzed and decisions can be made. If you skip a step here and make decisions without the needed information (or worse, if you have bad information), your decisions are destined to go bad.

CLOSE THE GAP

1. Describe how "managing up" looks in your world. How much of your professional energy is required? How would you assess your effort and time expenditure in managing up?

2. Has your boss (board, clientele) found you worthy of trust? How have you proven yourself to be valuable and nearly indispensible? Where have you fallen short in this area?

3. Consider a situation in which you over-promised. What effect did it have on your co-workers? Your boss? Did your adjustments afterward help to restore trust? How so?

_____

_____

_____

_____

4. Do you exhibit the quiet confidence that says you are competent and positioned to perform? How can you improve in this area? What confidence-building steps have you already taken?

_____

_____

_____

_____

5. Are you comfortable *not* being the smartest person in the room? How might insecurities in this area be serving to limit your professional growth? What steps can you take to gain increased exposure to those from whom you can learn?

_____

_____

_____

_____

6. How clearly are expectations conveyed and received in your organization? Do staffers leave meetings with "hearts and minds clear"? Why or why not? What remedies will you offer?

_____

_____

_____

_____

7. How would you rate your performance as a problem-solver? (Substantiate your response with recent examples.) To what degree have you empowered others to solve problems?

_____

_____

_____

_____

Chapter 6

Freedom: It's What the Leader Really Needs From You

A s you have worked through this book, you have un-
doubtedly noticed that I am a big believer that for any
organization to reach its full potential the leader has
to be free. The leader has to be free to do what he or she does
best. The leader has to be free to focus on the big, important
issues. The leader also has to be free to get away and relax.

In order for the leader to have that freedom, a few
things have to happen. First, the leader has to want for it
to happen. This is where the process stops before it ever
begins for most leaders. As discussed previously, they are
unwilling to let go. Maybe they don't have the right support team. Maybe they feel like only they can do it right.
Whatever the reason, a leader who insists on doing everything will be limited—because you can only do so much.

**A leader who insists on doing everything
will be limited—you can only do so much.**

The simple truth is to be able to grab onto what is in store for you, you have to be able to let go of some things from the past. You need to have a clear understanding of not only what you do best but also what is most effective. So take the first step, recognize that you need help, and follow the steps in this book to get it.

The next thing that needs to happen is that the leader needs to assemble the right team, develop trust in that team, and empower the team.

When the leader has a trusted team in place, he or she can start to enjoy the benefits of the freedom that he or she really needs in order to effectively manage and direct the whole organization. The leadership team then needs to understand that as they do their respective jobs, freedom for the boss is their goal. If the team understands that and acts accordingly, they will naturally do their jobs well.

Why is freedom for the leader so important not only to the survival of the organization but also to the ability of the organization to thrive?

First, in order for any organization to survive and thrive, there has to be a visionary at the top. When you have a visionary at the top and the visionary has *time* to behave like a visionary, the organization will have that all-important rudder to guide its direction. Look at what I just said. The leader has to have time to be a visionary and he or she has to behave like a visionary. In all organizations, but in religious organizations specifically, this is hugely important. The leader of the religious organization by definition must be in concert with God's will and desire for the organization. That means the leader must be *free* to spend the time it takes to behave like a visionary. This means the time to study, pray, and think about where the organization is headed, what the organization is doing, and how it is managing its resources.

The leader can't accomplish this objective if he or she is spending all of his or her time trying tend to the myriad details of running a growing organization. It also means that you can't be a visionary if you have other people to run the organization but you don't let them do their jobs.

A closely related point is that your team will know whether or not the leader truly is a visionary leader. If the team recognizes that their leader truly has a vision for the organization, there is no better motivation. People will roll up their sleeves and fight and sweat and bleed for something they believe in. If the leader knows where he or she is going and everyone else buys into that vision, there is no limit to the possibility. The flip side is true as well. If the team begins to understand that the leader doesn't have a true calling and vision, the extraordinary effort will not be there. All of a sudden, you will have people who are simply doing a job, nothing more. It is the extraordinary effort and dedication that comes from fulfilling a purpose that creates the opportunity for a result that has been blessed.

Being free also means that the leader has the opportunity to focus on other critical areas of leadership. For example, I have previously discussed the focus that is needed on identifying and developing people in your organization. Just as vision requires time to study, pray, and think, developing your people requires an investment of time. The leader has to be able to interact with his or her team in a positive manner. There has to be interaction outside of, "Is that done?" You have to be able to observe and guide the decision-making and leadership skills of your top people. You have to have good information— what people do well and don't do well, what motivates and inspires them, how far can you stretch them without breaking them, and most importantly, how you as a leader can best help them advance their own careers. It all takes time, and time requires freedom.

Finally, being free means the ability to have and maintain a balanced life. All leaders, but particularly pastors, are prone to burnout. Moreover, the extreme demands of a busy professional life can lead to problematic personal lives. Both burnout and problems at home can often be remedied by finding a better, more equitable balance. Here again, the critical issue is time. If the leader knows and has confidence that the team is performing and taking care of business, the leader can relax and spend some needed time focusing on other areas of his or her life, like spending time with his or her family, taking a vacation, or simply getting away from the problems that world presents every day.

If you are a leader, make it your goal and objective to build the team that gives you the freedom you need. If you are one of the team members, make sure everyone on the team knows how important it is for the leader to have freedom. Everyone will benefit from it.

CLOSE THE GAP

1. Are you/your leader enjoying the freedom that is needed to focus on the big, important issues? Explain your response.

_____

_____

_____

_____

Section 3

Speaking to Everyone

Chapter 7

Building on a Solid Foundation

Just as identifying, hiring, managing, and motivating the right team is an essential element to filling the leadership gap, so too is having a proper corporate structure and foundation for your organization to work within. While this is not intended to be and is not a legal guide, a brief discussion of the proper structure for your organization can be beneficial.

If your organization has not already done so, the first step in establishing your foundation is to set up and properly structure a nonprofit corporation through which your organization will operate. As a bit of background, an organization is simply a legal entity that the law has created so that a group of people can operate a common enterprise together for a common objective. The law allows for people to form an entity, called a corporation, so that the enterprise—be it a church, oil company, or a car wash—can have its own existence, separate and apart from the people who operate the enterprise.

**A corporation has its own existence
separate and apart from the people who
operate the enterprise.**

The separate existence provides the corporation with two distinct advantages. First, the corporation will provide you with personal legal protection against liability. Because the corporation has a separate legal existence, this provides a distinction between the entity and the people who run it. As a general matter, the corporation and not the people who operate the corporation are liable and accountable for any actions of the corporation. In other words, the corporation acts as a legal shield of protection for the individuals involved in running it. The bottom line is that, rather than you being sued personally if your corporation were, for example, to breach a contract, the corporation would be sued and not you.

Here's a quick example. Assume that the church bus is involved in an accident. The accident was caused by Pastor Brown, a church employee, and Bob Jones, the driver of the other vehicle involved in the accident, is seriously injured and incurred several thousands of dollars in medical bills and is off work for six months. Bob Jones is going to want someone to pay for his injury and lost wages. Without the protection of a corporation, Pastor Wilson, who runs the church but was nowhere near the accident, as well as Pastor Brown, who caused the accident, are more likely to be the ones who get sued by Bob Jones. However, if a corporation exists, it will be the corporation, not the individuals, which typically would get sued.

Similar rules will apply to the debts and obligations of the nonprofit organization. If the corporation incurred debts, the corporation alone is liable for those debts (unless some individual personally guaranteed the debt obligation). Clearly, the separate existence and legal shield afforded by forming a corporation is beneficial and serves to protect the individuals involved in running the organization.

Incorporation affords a legal shield that protects the individuals involved in running the organization.

The next reason to form a nonprofit corporation for your organization is that it will make it much easier for your organization to enjoy the benefits and advantages of being tax exempt. While it is possible for a church or other ministry to operate on a tax-exempt basis without forming a corporation, it is often increasingly difficult. Businesses and governmental agencies particularly are used to dealing with corporate entities. By forming the nonprofit corporation, you have made it very clear what your organization is. In addition, you will find that filing for and obtaining various exemptions for sales taxes, property taxes, and the like will be greatly eased.

One quick related point here. It needs to be noted that churches, unlike ministries and other nonprofit organizations, are not required to make any filings with the federal government to be deemed tax exempt. Churches, in fact, are deemed to be automatically tax exempt by the Internal Revenue Service and are not required to file a form 1023 as an application for recognition of their exempt status. However, non-church ministries and other nonprofit corporations are in fact required to file the form 1023 with the Internal Revenue Service and apply for recognition of their exempt status.

Based on the foregoing, it is easy to see and understand why it is to the benefit of both you and your organization to create a nonprofit organization under which your church or ministry will be operated. That being said, it is worthy of a brief discussion regarding how to best set up and structure the corporation as well as a few tips on maintaining the corporation in order to ensure it continues to provide you with the benefits for which it was intended.

STRUCTURING THE CORPORATION

The actual process of creating or forming the corporation is very simple. You can either hire a lawyer to manage the process for you or, if the budget is in extreme consideration, you may want to consider forming the corporation yourself. Most states' secretary of state websites contain all of the proper forms and information that you would need to actually create and form the entity.

Filing the actual formation documents with the secretary of state in your state is a relatively simple process. However, the more involved and complicated process is in the setting up of the actual bylaws of the organization.

The bylaws are the single most important document for governance of the corporation. Essentially, the bylaws set forth the rules for corporate governance and establish who exactly is empowered to do what with regards to actions taken by the corporation.

—————◆•◆•◆—————

The bylaws are the single most important document for governance of the corporation.

—————◆•◆•◆—————

Given recent events over the last few years where a number of founders of high-profile, nonprofit corporations have been removed from the leadership of their respective organizations, it is worth a brief discussion regarding the bylaws and a few considerations in how those documents should be structured.

First, it is important to note that there are essentially three different corporate structures that most organizations follow. First is the board-run organization, which either does not have members or if it does, the members have no authority to vote on matters of corporate governance. In this type of structure, all of the ultimate corporate authority rests with the board of directors. In this type of situation, any limits on the power of the board of directors would need to be set forth in the organization's bylaws.

The second typical corporate structure for nonprofits is what is referred to as a member-managed organization.

In these organizations, rather than the board of directors, it is actually the members of the organization who ultimately hold final authority. For example, the bylaws of such an organization would specify certain acts or actions of the corporation, which would require the consent of the members, and in addition it would be the members who are responsible for electing the board of directors. In turn, the board of directors would elect the officers of the organization, who would in fact be responsible for the day-to-day management and operation of the entity. The differences between a member-run organization and a board-run organizations are primarily that: 1) the member-run organization is generally required to hold a vote of its members to approve certain types of actions or to incur certain obligations, and 2) the members would typically be responsible for electing the board of directors. However, in a board-run organization, it is the board of directors themselves who typically would elect the board of directors.

The third type of organizational structure would be a hybrid of the board-run and member-run organizations. In this circumstance, members would typically have less authority than in a member-run organization, but the board of directors would be subject to the will of the members for certain specified actions.

The important point here is that your bylaws need to accurately and correctly set forth the type of structure under which you want your organization to operate. Then, on a go-forward basis, you need to ensure that you are in fact operating your organization in accordance with the rules and procedures set forth in the bylaws.

————◆•◆•◆————

Your bylaws need to accurately set forth the structure under which you want your organization to operate.

————◆•◆•◆————

Maintaining a Corporation

Now that you've decided to set up your nonprofit corporation and you've had discussions and made a decision regarding the type of corporate structure you want to have, you can have your organization formed and begin to operate as a corporation. On a go-forward basis, in order to maintain your corporate status, there are a few simple steps that you will need to follow.

1. You will need to maintain the separateness of the corporation.

What this means is that you must not operate the corporation as if you and the corporation are one in the same. In other words, the corporation should have its own checking and savings accounts, its own books and records, and the corporation's checking account should not be treated as if it is your own checking account. In other words, you need to take care of personal matters with personal funds and corporate matters with corporate funds.

2. You need to ensure that you have both board meetings and/or business meetings of your membership (if required to by your corporate structure)

on a regular basis as set forth in your corporate bylaws.

Those actions that require a vote of either the board of directors or the membership should in fact be taken to either the board of directors or the membership as applicable. The individuals (or the officers) of the organization should not take actions that require either board or member approval without first gaining that approval.

3. You need to make sure that your corporation promptly files any forms that are required by your state.

For instance, many states require nonprofit corporations to file public information reports listing officers and directors. If you fail to file the reports in a timely manner, your status as a valid corporation can be forfeited and lost. So the bottom line is to simply make sure that you respond to any notices from the state on time.

One gap in the leadership of many nonprofit organizations is that the leadership fails to identify, recruit, and properly utilize qualified board members who can add value to the organization.

VALUABLE BOARD MEMBERS

While this topic will be discussed in greater detail in the chapter regarding community involvement, it should be noted that board members can be, and should be, a valued and valuable part of a management leadership team. Specifically, you should be looking for board members who can assist and add value to your organization in the following ways.

1. Fundraising

Your board of directors should be a valuable resource for the organization when it comes to fundraising. Not only should the board members themselves ideally be generous donors and give to the organization, but they should also be helpful to you by identifying other persons who are likely to support whatever your cause or activity might be.

2. Experience

Generally speaking, you will want to identify and recruit experienced and savvy people to sit on your board of directors. As a result, members of your board will often either have business or life experience that is highly relevant and applicable to your organization's particular activities. In this respect, your board of directors should act as a resource to your leadership team. That is to say that as you embark upon a new endeavor or a new initiative, you should take time to check in with your board members and find out who, if anyone on the board, has experience or knowledge that relates to whatever your undertaking may be. In many cases, you will find that you will save yourself and/or your staff valuable time, effort, and money by being able to identify potential hazards as well as potential opportunities as you go forth with your initiative.

**Your board of directors should act as a
resource to your leadership team.**

One last point with regard to setting the proper foundation, corporately, for your organization is that it is in this process in establishing your foundation that you will be afforded the opportunity to properly protect not only yourself but also your employees and your board members. In order to get the most out of your employees as well as your board members, those individuals need to know and understand that in the course of acting in their official capacity on behalf of the organization, the organization is going to stand behind and protect them. Having board members and employees who know that they are free to act and know that they have backup protection will help to motivate them and inspire them to deliver to their fullest.

This protection is afforded to them through indemnification and insurance. Indemnification, very simply, is an agreement (usually set forth in the bylaws of the organization) whereby the organization agrees to be responsible for any actions of its employees, officers, or board members that were undertaken in good faith while acting in their official capacities. Going back to our example of the church bus accident, if the organization has proper indemnification procedures, then Pastor Jones who caused the auto accident will know that it is the corporation and not himself that will ultimately be responsible.

As a general matter, the indemnification obligations of the organization are then in turn backed up by insurance. In addition to the typical liability insurance that most organizations would maintain, it's advisable to maintain coverage to protect your officers and directors from liability for actions they may take on behalf of the organization. Through a proper combination of insurance and indemnification, your officers, board members, and other employees can rest more easily knowing that they are protected against liability that they may incur as a result of acting on behalf of the organization. Having such protection in place will serve to not only allow you to attract better and more qualified people, but it will also motivate those people to be willing to act in the manner that they truly believe to be in the best interest of the corporation, as apposed to acting in the manner that they feel will expose them to the least amount of liability.

In summary, having the proper corporate structure (and following that structure) and effectively recruiting, protecting, and utilizing board members will set the solid foundation that your organization needs to build on. Without this solid foundation, you may find that the sands have shifted under you when a crisis arises.

CLOSE THE GAP

1. Describe a scenario in which your organization would benefit (or already benefits) from the separate existence and legal shield afforded by

incorporation. How would the absence of this structure impact the organization and its staff?

_____

_____

_____

_____

_____

2. Must you file IRS Form 1023 for your organization to be tax-exempt? Why or why not?

_____

_____

_____

_____

3. Which type of corporate structure best serves the needs of your organization? Explain.

_____

_____

_____

_____

_____

4. In what practical ways do you separate yourself from the corporate entity? Describe a misstep that could cause you to forfeit incorporation.

_____

_____

_____

_____

5. If you already have a board of directors, take a moment to assess in writing the value each director adds to your organization. If you are considering a future board, whom do you consider to be good candidates, and why?

_____

_____

_____

_____

6. Are the good-faith actions taken in the course of official business by your organization's employees, officers, or board members adequately indemnified? Explain.

_____

_____

_____

_____

7. How do such protections serve to attract and empower staffers to act in the best interests of the organization?

_____

_____

_____

_____

Chapter 8

The Power of Community Involvement

Oddly enough, community involvement is one area in which almost all churches, ministries, and nonprofits tend to fall short. I am not sure why this is, except maybe that this is a case similar to the plumber who has a house with leaky pipes or the painter whose house needs painting. Perhaps people who spend their days and careers working for ministries and other nonprofits are somehow reluctant to spend their volunteer time on behalf of another similar organization.

In my opinion, this is a huge missed opportunity. Both leaders and their senior staffs should all find meaningful ways to become involved in community organizations in their area. Once you begin to go down this road, you will begin to see many of the substantial benefits that can result to both you personally and your organization as a result of this involvement.

BENEFITS

The first benefit is one that is purely selfish. By being involved in community organizations outside of your own, you are given an excellent opportunity to meet with others and talk about and discuss what is going on in your own organization. It is just simply part of human nature that as soon as you get to know people outside of your own group, you will naturally share what it is that you do and how your organization is involved in the community and the different things that you are doing. And by involving yourself with other community organizations, you will inevitably be exposing both yourself and your own organization to your community's most influential and prominent people.

Involvement with other community organizations will expose you to influential and prominent people.

This certainly has been the case with regard to my personal involvement, outside of The Potter's House, with Parkland Hospital (the public hospital located in the city of Dallas). Through my time both on the board of directors of the Parkland Foundation and later my years of service on the Dallas County Blue Ribbon Commission of Parkland Hospital, I got to know a number of Dallas' most influential business and political leaders.

One of the interesting results of this involvement in this experience was that I discovered how many people were aware of and interested in Mission Jinks and The Potter's House but had no real knowledge or understanding of what we did, what our interests were, and the ways in which we were impacting the greater community. Accordingly, as a result of getting to know these people over several years, I was able to not only expand my personal network of business and political relationships but also to expand the reach of The Potter's House by enabling others outside The Potter's House to get a better understanding of what we did and what our goals and objectives were.

Another tremendous benefit of community involvement is that such involvements, particularly on a high level, will broaden your views and expose you to new and different ideas that could be potentially applied to the management of your own organization. As we all know, each individual organization has its own rhythm, its own culture, and its own philosophy with regard to how it conducts its business and other activities on a day-to-day basis. The only real way to get exposed to these different viewpoints is to have experience with another organization in a manner that is up close and personal.

For example, the Parkland Foundation has been extremely successful in raising donated funds for a tax-appointed hospital. As a result of being involved in this process, I've gained valuable insights and expertise as to how an organization outside of the church world can go about raising substantial funds. Clearly, this experience and exposure has enabled me to bring new concepts and ideas to the organization I am involved with on a day-to-day basis.

Community involvement will broaden your views and expose you to new and different ideas.

In addition to being able to witness those things that work effectively and being able to apply those to your own organization, you will also be able to witness and observe some things that in fact don't work as well. These experiences can be just as valuable to your organization as the information that you learned from the success of the organization in which you were involved.

As well as learning from the successes and failures of the agencies in which you choose to involve yourself, you can also benefit from the more subtle lessons available to you simply in terms of the philosophy, culture, and approach that is taken by an organization. Here, the list of potential benefits can be endless. For example, you may involve yourself in a community organization that has a tremendous way to motivate their employees or is particularly skilled at dealing with the press or other outside influences.

One of the most rewarding aspects of community involvement is when you're able to apply your own business experience and skills in ways that are beneficial and additive to the organization that you have chosen to volunteer for. For example, in TDJ Enterprises one of our strengths is clearly marketing. During my time working with Parkland Hospital, it became clearly evident that one of the weaknesses of Parkland was their ability to market themselves and discuss the positive thing they were doing in the community. As a result, greater effort was made in that area, and significant focus was given toward informing the community as a whole about the efforts and the work undertaken by Parkland Hospital. The final result was that during the recession, Parkland Hospital was able to get voter approval of a bond package to build a new $1.3 billion hospital that required a tax increase with the support of over 80 percent of the voters.

RELATIONSHIPS

The next major benefit of community involvement is quite simply the power of the relationships and the contacts you will develop over time. During my work with Parkland, I have developed strong business, medical, and political contacts that have all proven extremely useful in my other work on behalf of The Potter's House and TDJ Enterprises.

For example, one of my contacts through Parkland is also on the Texas Commission for the Arts, and she has been extremely helpful in assisting us to work with the governor's office of the state of Texas and other organizations to assist us in bringing increased film and television activity into the state of Texas.

These relationships can be hugely beneficial on a very personal and practical level.

Because I have had such deep involvement with a major hospital tied to a major medical school, I now have significant contacts in the Dallas medical community. These types of relationships can be hugely beneficial on a very personal and practical level. For example, as a result of my contacts at Parkland, I have been able to get top-tier medical assistance for employees as well as other friends and personal relationships during times of personal need for them. When someone is undergoing a medical crisis, there is nothing quite so comforting as to be able to make sure that you have the attention of the CEO of the hospital in making sure that your friend or loved one is getting the proper care and attention he or she deserves. Moreover, this has been able to extend well beyond the reaches of Parkland Hospital itself. For example, when I've had friends or loved ones who are in other hospitals around the city, my contacts at Parkland have always been able to get me in touch with the right people at the applicable hospital.

Here's another great example of the power of the relationships that can be built through community involvement. A good friend of mine was recently experiencing a financial crisis and was having difficulty working with his bank in regard to his mortgage loan. The bank had approved a modification to this friend's mortgage but then later retracted the offer for modification. My friend was having tremendous difficulty working though the bureaucracy of this large national bank. Because of contacts developed with the senior executives at that bank through my community involvement, I was able to, in a very short amount of time, contact senior executives in the bank who were able to get the correct people involved in and looking at my friend's particular circumstance. The end result is that the friend, whose home at the time we discussed it was in foreclosure, has now been able to rework his loan with his lender, stay in his home, and everyone from my friend to the bank is happy with the end result.

You simply cannot overvalue the importance and the benefits of developing significant relationships in the business and political worlds. By investing and developing these contacts, you are often able to achieve more beneficial results with less investment of time and money on your behalf. There is simply nothing like being able to pick up the phone, have a conversation, and solve a problem in a few minutes that could otherwise take days or even months to rectify through normal channels.

Investing and developing these contacts produces beneficial results with less time and money.

So the bottom line is that both you and your senior staff need to become involved in meaningful community organizations in your area. To get this done requires both support for top leadership as well as an emphasis and a willingness to invest the time and effort that is required for this involvement. One important note here—the decision to become involved in a community organization is an important and significant one. Once you go down this path, it is something you need to follow through on and make sure it is managed in a proper manner. Nothing will reflect quite so badly on your organization as having members of your senior staff starting down the road to being involved in these organizations and then quickly becoming the absentee member of the board. Such an approach will only serve to create negative impressions of both you and your organization in the broader community. As a result, there needs to be a conscious decision by management that this is important. There has to be a decision that each senior staff member will be given the time and the freedom necessary to properly involve him or herself in the appropriate organization.

One final note here with regard to community involvement. It is my strong recommendation that you attempt to focus your involvement, to the degree possible, in becoming involved in community organizations at a high level. Ideally, both you and your members of your senior staff will serve on the board of directors of multiple organizations. While your involvement at the grass-roots level of these organizations is something that will be personally beneficial and will be great for the community, it is not going to provide you or your organization with the significant benefits discussed above. The significant business and political relationships as well as knowledge of the inner workings of these organizations, is, as a general matter, going to come from service on their board of directors or otherwise being involved in the organization's higher levels.

CLOSE THE GAP

1. Assess the degree to which your organization is involved in the community. To what do you attribute this level of involvement?

   _____

   _____

   _____

   _____

2. What "selfish" benefits of community involvement have accrued to (or been missed by) your organization? Give specifics.

    _____

    _____

    _____

    _____

3. How has your organization's learning curve (operationally speaking) been shortened through community involvement? What benefits might result from increased involvement?

    _____

    _____

    _____

    _____

4. How has your organization gleaned (or how might it glean in the future) from the cultures or philosophies of other entities? How might this interaction prove mutually beneficial?

    _____

    _____

    _____

    _____

5. How can your organization and members benefit from the relationships formed through community involvement? Describe one or two firsthand experiences that illustrate this concept.

_____

_____

_____

_____

6. Can you identify any conditions that hinder your organization from becoming more involved in the community? How can these adverse conditions be resolved?

_____

_____

_____

_____

7. Is your organization involved with other entities at a high level? What is the benefit of high-level rather than grass-roots involvement? What adjustments can you make along these lines?

_____

_____

_____

_____

Chapter 9

Doing Business

Over the last half century, the dynamics of operating churches, ministries, and other nonprofit corporations have changed dramatically. Advances in the fields of radio, television, publishing, the Internet, and entertainment have made it possible for the leader of a local organization to reach an audience of incredible size and scope. For example, the seating capacity of the local church sanctuary no longer dictates the size of the audience that may be reached by the Sunday message. Today, a pastor standing alone in a television studio can reach an audience far larger than the crowd addressed by the pastor standing before tens of thousands in a football stadium. Today, through the use of technology, it is possible to reach a significant portion of the world's population at any given time. In this environment, it is no surprise that many of today's ministry leaders are starting to compete with Hollywood's elite in terms of the audience that they reach.

In fact, recent statistics show that over 170 million Americans attend some type of church service on a weekly basis. This is an audience, in terms of size and scope, that Hollywood only dreams about. By comparison, the moviegoing audience for a given week is only 15 to 25 million people (depending on how big the movies are opening that weekend). That means that America's churches reach an audience that is seven to ten times the size of the audience the movie studios reach on any given weekend. As a result, more and more ministry organizations are using the tools of media conglomerates to more effectively and cost efficiently reach and communicate with a vast audience available to them. In turn, effective use of the available media leads to a level of exposure that causes the individuals who lead the media ministries to obtain unprecedented levels of exposure and attention.

America's churches reach an audience seven to ten times the size of the weekend moviegoing audience.

At the same time, advances in technology and distribution are now making it possible for smaller and smaller organizations to begin the process of effectively reaching the masses. The end result is that more and more ministers, ministries, and nonprofit organizations are having to prepare to deal with the realities of the entertainment economy.

In today's world, a myriad of entertainment-related opportunities are available to ministries in a way they were never available before. In many cases, these opportunities are best dealt with outside of the corporate structure of the ministry or nonprofit organization. That being the case, this chapter will provide you with basic information on how to deal with and effectively manage business opportunities that may come to your leadership separate and apart from the organization itself.

NONPROFIT OR FOR-PROFIT?

Whether it's in the form of books or music or movies or even blogging, you should consider setting up these separate business opportunities in a corporation or entity outside of the structure of your nonprofit organization. While it is the initial inclination of many ministry and nonprofit leaders to conduct personal business through their existing nonprofit, it's often better to set up a separate for-profit entity for these ventures.

It's often better to set up a separate for-profit entity for entertainment-related ventures.

In making this evaluation, you first need to remember what a nonprofit corporation is and is not. A nonprofit corporation is not owned by anyone. In reality, a nonprofit corporation is effectively owned by the public at large and the state has the right to ensure that its assets are used only for nonprofit purposes. On the other hand, a for-profit company is owned by its shareholders, and this means that the shareholders can do what they wish with the company and its assets. In other words, even if you control a nonprofit corporation, its assets are not owned by you. On the other hand, if you control a for-profit corporation, in fact you do own and control its assets as a practical matter. The important distinction here is often in the issue of your estate and providing for your descendants. While you can leave your descendants all of the stock in your for-profit corporation, you cannot will them control of a nonprofit.

This whole discussion is probably best illustrated with a simple example. Let's assume that Pastor Johnson has a large, growing church. In addition, he is beginning to get requests to speak at conferences, conventions, and church gatherings around the country, and has drawn the attention of a major book publisher as well as a movie studio. Let's assume that Pastor Johnson decides to enter into a contract with the publisher through the nonprofit organization instead of through a separate company that he only owns. The following would be the result.

First, the nonprofit organization will receive the advance, if any, and the royalties earned by the book. While it's true that the nonprofit will not pay any tax on the compensation that it receives from the sale of the book, any money from the book sale that the organization pays to Pastor Johnson would be compensation that would trigger two things. First, all the money paid to Pastor Johnson would be income to him and taxed at ordinary income rates. Second, the payments to Pastor Johnson would be considered part of his total compensation from the nonprofit and must meet the requirements of reasonableness. While at certain income levels this might not be an issue, if Pastor Johnson's ministry grows and the book succeeds and earns significant royalty income, Pastor Johnson may not be able to receive all the compensation that may flow from the book because he will get to the point where his total compensation from the church exceeds the amount which would otherwise be deemed reasonable. Moreover, the nonprofit will now own the copyright to the book, a very valuable asset. This means that Pastor Johnson's children cannot inherit the copyright. Worse, if Pastor Johnson were to ever leave the nonprofit, he would not be able to take the copyright with him without compensating the organization for the copyright.

So the results here are easy enough to judge. Pastor Johnson will still pay taxes on all the compensation he receives from the nonprofit, he will not own the valuable asset in terms of the intellectual property of the copyright of the book, and that asset cannot become a legacy to his family unless he purchases it back from the non profit at some point at full fair market value. On the other hand, if Pastor Johnson had created a for-profit entity—call it Pastor Johnson Incorporated—the result would have been much more beneficial to him personally. All of the advances and royalties would be paid to his corporation, without any question as to the reasonableness of the amount. The income would still be taxable, just as if it were paid to him by the church. However, through his ownership of the corporation, Pastor Johnson would have opened up tax and estate planning opportunities, and more importantly the copyright of the book can be fully controlled and transferred to others, including family members.

As a result, personal business opportunities, when structured in a separate business, can not only open up the potential for increased unrestricted income and the possibility of creating a legacy for your family, but just as importantly they can open up venues for your creative efforts. By their nature, most ministry leaders are creative people; be it writing and delivering a sermon or writing and singing a song, the process of ministry is often a creative one. It is true that most creative people need multiple outlets through which they can breathe life into their creative thoughts and inspirations.

Separately structured businesses can open up unrestricted income, a family legacy, and creative venues.

Very often, some of your best investments may be those investments you make in your own creative thoughts and ideas. Even an individual or a ministry with limited financial resources can invest its time, energy, and money to create a new book, song, play, or some other concept. Once that vision becomes real, numerous opportunities exist for the exploitation of the creation.

So clearly, ample reasons exist for many ministry and nonprofit leaders to form their own separate business entities. Accordingly, the discussion moves from how to order the entity to how to maximize the entity's opportunities and minimize risk.

Opportunity and Risk

The primary liability concern is the embroilment of IRS entanglement. The IRS has two principle concerns in regards to your business: 1) whether your business properly reports income and pays its taxes (the same concern it has with every other person and business in the United States), and 2) whether the dealings between your company and your ministry or nonprofit are fair and reasonable.

The first concern is common to everyone and will not be addressed here, except to say that you should find a competent CPA to assist you with tax and financial planning.

On the second issue, all the IRS rules with regard to private interest and excess benefits apply to dealings between your ministry or nonprofit and your separate business. This means that 1) you cannot use nonprofit assets for the benefit of your personal business without paying fair compensation for the use of those assets, and 2) any business arrangements or transactions between your business and your related ministry or nonprofit must be fair and reasonable.

Continuing the example with Pastor Johnson, consider two points. First, if Pastor Johnson uses his secretary to type the transcript of his book, the church must be compensated for the use of her services or the service must be valued and added upon Pastor Johnson's compensation. Why is this necessary? The church secretary is paid by the church, and therefore her time during regular church business hours belongs to the ministry and should not be used for private activities unless the church is compensated. Therefore, Pastor Johnson should hire someone outside the church or ensure the church is properly compensated or identify a volunteer to help him with his typing efforts.

This issue of separateness can be very problematic in practice. Therefore, if Pastor Johnson's business is significant enough to justify it, the pastor should set up a totally separate office with a separate staff, separate credit arrangements, separate accounting, and the like to ensure that the separateness is maintained. Until you reach this point, however, you will simply need to be careful to maintain separateness between the activities of the nonprofit and your personal business activities.

Be careful to maintain separateness between nonprofit and personal business activities.

The next issue is the question of fairness between any transactions that take place between your business and your nonprofit. Such transactions are common for ministers and others who are engaged in music or other writing activities. For example, most publishing contracts allow the author to purchase copies of the work from the publisher at decently discounted prices (such as 60 to 80 percent off the retail price of the book) and then re-sell those copies in specified (usually non-retail) sales channels. Given this ability to buy and re-sell books, it is very attractive for all parties involved for the ministry leader/author to purchase and re-sell copies of his book to the ministry for re-sell. Such an arrangement is perfectly fine, so long as the business deal itself is fair. In this case, the nonprofit needs to get as good a deal or better than it could get otherwise. For example, if the ministry would be able to buy the books from a distributor for a 45 percent discount, it would be improper for the organization to buy the books from its ministry leader at only a 40 percent discount. However, a deal to buy a 45 percent or better discount would be perfectly legitimate.

In summary, if the deal is fair and separateness is maintained, you will go a long way toward assuring that neither organization will be put in jeopardy.

EMPLOYMENT

A related point in regard to the business activities of the leader of a nonprofit is the importance of having an effective employment agreement in place. The employment agreement would not only define issues such as compensation, under what circumstances the employee can be dismissed, and the consequences of dismissing the employee, but it will also help address the issues like who owns what in regard to intellectual property. As discussed above, in the ministry world most of the leaders are inherently creative and are constantly in the process of creating new intellectual property. It is through an effective employment agreement that the ownership and rights with regard to this intellectual property are best established.

Why is this important? Under copyright law, there is a concept known as "work made for hire." Essentially what this means is that the creative works of the employee created in the course of the employee's work are, absent a separate written agreement to the contrary, generally considered to be the product or the works of the employer. In other words, the concept is that since the employer is paying for you and that you created the work while being paid by the employer, the employer would own the benefits of the work. It is through the employer agreement, however, that the "work made for hire" concept can be addressed and can be clarified so that the employee and not the organization is the owner of his or her intellectual property or creations.

One of the most important capabilities of any nonprofit leader and the leadership team is the ability to say no.

BUSINESS OPPORTUNITIES

As any leader moves from the nonprofit world into the business world, it will be important to carefully consider the opportunities that are made available to you. The best advice I can give you is to simply do what you do. What I mean is simply this. Business ventures that take advantage of your unique gifts and talents are far more likely to be successful than business ventures that do not. When you look at an opportunity or a venture, carefully consider what you are bringing to the table. This will tell you if you are just an investor in the transaction or if you have some special position or ability to add value to the overall transaction.

The next related point is that in all ventures in which you decide to undertake, you need to consider very carefully the impact and ramifications of brand management. Every venture and opportunity on which you embark will have some impact upon the brand of you and/or your organization. Accordingly, you need to ensure the opportunities upon which you decide to embark are those that will have a positive reflection and be additive toward your brand.

One of the real skills you and your team will need to develop over time is the ability to sort through the opportunities that become available to you and to select only those opportunities that are a positive reflection on your brand, have the greatest potential for success, and are the best fit for you and your organization. In the course of my work as the chief operating officer of TDJ Enterprises, I am constantly being inundated with proposals that stretch the gamut of multi-million dollar deals with Fortune 500 companies to proposals from Sister Susie who makes cookies in her kitchen at home. Whether you want to or not, you are going to need to develop a system for responding to these inquires.

Select only those opportunities that reflect positively on your brand and fit your organization and mission.

When you are approached with new deals every day like we are at TDJ Enterprises, you have to be able to quickly and effectively separate the real deals from the dogs. A big part of my job is to evaluate the potential offers and bring forward those opportunities that make sense and have significant potential. As you look at and examine potential business opportunities, consider the following points.

1. Consider the source.

Did this proposal or idea come from a reliable, known, or confident source? Did the prospective deal come to you through someone who you know, trust, or respect? There are a number of people I have tremendous respect for through the business community. That respect has been earned over years, so I am not wasting my time. If someone I respect brings an opportunity to my attention, I will always take the time to carefully consider and evaluate their proposal. I may still say no but not before I've adequately checked it out. On the other hand, the multitude of opportunities that come to me through unknown or un-trusted sources already have at least two strikes against them.

You need to remember, time is too precious to waste. You need to spend your time and energy on those opportunities that have a greater chance for success.

In this respect, the source of materials and opportunities is important. Credible people and credible opportunities, if they do not have a direct connection to you, will find other creditable people through which to approach you. As a result, those things that come to you through dubious or unknown sources likely should be dismissed.

2. Choose long-term partners.

Real success is rarely achieved the first time you do something. The real results are more likely to be built over time. This means that you need business partners who are in business for the long term. Short-term partners are inevitably after a quick buck and lack the integrity, ability, and stamina to work a project over the long term to ensure its success.

Finding such partners is easier said than done, but it is critically important. The integrity, commitment, and knowledge of your partners are often more important to your long-term success than the up-front numbers on the contract. For example, you can get the greatest book deal in the world, with a big advance and a great royalty rate, but if your publisher decides not to aggressively market your book, your long-term value as an author will be diminished because you (not the publisher) will be labeled as an author who didn't sell. That means you need to take as much time to evaluate the quality of your partners as you do the quality of the deal. Simply going with the highest bidder on a transaction may not be the most beneficial long-term course of action.

Going with the highest bidder may not be the most beneficial long-term course of action.

When you are evaluating a potential deal, you need to consider the likely outcomes. One of three things will happen when you enter into a new business relationship—it will either go great, it will go badly, or it will do just OK. In two of those circumstances, integrity is key. If the deal goes good, a partner that lacks integrity and gets greedy may think they should be entitled to more than what the contract provides. When the deal goes bad, partners that lack integrity will start to fight or cause other distractions in an attempt to not have to pay up on a legitimate loss.

Accordingly, when you are evaluating a potential deal, one of the important things to attempt to judge is the integrity and commitment of your partners. While this can be a difficult thing to judge, your instincts can be an invaluable resource. If your potential partner tries to keep moving the deal around before you even have a deal, he will probably try to do the same after you have the deal, especially in success. In the few cases in my career where I've found myself fighting too hard to get the deal done in the first place, I have usually lived to regret it. I do not mean that deals and transactions should not be heavily and fiercely negotiated; they should. Some of my toughest negotiations were with people for whom I have tremendous respect and with whom I will always want to do business. This is the way that the world should work. However common, what I am talking about is the potential partner who is clearly trying to take advantage and has that sort of "sleaze" that permeates all that they do. Bottom line—if you don't sense integrity during the negotiations, then it's certainly not going to be there in the performance of the deal.

----◆•◆•◆----

If you don't sense integrity during negotiations, it won't be there in the performance of the deal.

----◆•◆•◆----

This means that you need to spend some time check-ing out your potential business partners. It can save you an awful lot of headaches. It is a simple truth that if someone stinks up enough offices, the stink usually can-not be hidden for long. While making calls to people you know in the industry this person has either done business with or attempted to do business with, you can get the real skinny pretty quickly. The bottom line is whether you can see yourself in a long-term business relationship or organization. It is just a simple truth that long-term relationships are more profitable than short-term ones, and it is simply not possible to have long-term relation-ships with short-term people.

3. The next question is whether or not the proposed business deal or transaction fits your mission or fits what you do.

Very simply, if you would need to adjust your vision or your mission to fit the deal, you should probably pass on the deal. More simply put, do what you do and leave the rest to someone else.

4. Does it fit on a napkin?

In my opinion, common good business arrangements should always be simple and make sense. If a deal involves elements you do not understand or are unfamiliar with, there is probably a problem. I'm not talking about all the legalese in a 50-page contract—working through the legalese is what lawyers are for. What I am talking about are the basic elements of the business deal itself. You should be able to reduce the deal to a picture on a nap-kin. Every deal should come down to, "I will do this, you will do that, I will get this, and you will get that." How you get there may be complicated, but the essence of the deal needs to be exactly that simple. If the deal does not in fact fit on a napkin, there is probably something wrong with it and you should move on.

———————

**You should be able to reduce a good
business deal to a picture on a napkin.**

———————

5.   Can you afford to fight with this partner?

You should be very careful about entering into business relationships with people you cannot afford to get into a fight with. We all want to maintain harmonious business relationships. That, however, is not always possible. Sometimes people just do the wrong thing. When that happens, you will try to resolve the problem. But if you can't resolve it, you have to choose. Are you going to fight, or are you going to accept the wrong that has been done to you? If you do business with someone who for some reason you cannot or should not get into a fight with, you lose options. When you lose options, the other side gains leverage.

This means that you need to be careful about doing business with family, prominent church members, donors, other organizational supporters, and anyone else who may be in a position to detrimentally impact your life separate and apart from the deal.

6.   Is this the best partner?

If you have determined that the deal is something that works for you and you want to get into the proposed business, consider whether the proposed business partner is the best possible partner for you. What does this partner bring to you that other partners cannot bring? Is this partner financially stable? Essentially, is there another potential partner that you should be considering? Over the years, I have had lots of people come to me with great ideas and concepts. The problem was that they didn't bring anything to the deal other than the idea. They didn't have any capacity to add value. That doesn't work. I need partners who bring significant value in exchange for their part of the deal.

———•◦•———

You need partners who bring not just ideas, but significant value in exchange for their part of the deal.

———•◦•———

At the end of the day, if the deal looks good and passes the tests set forth above, you may have something. At this point, I always advise people to seek a multitude of counsel and ask people with varied backgrounds and perspectives for their input. You never know who you may talk to who may have that one critical piece of information that helps you make the best possible decision. Quite simply, you cannot make great decisions without great information.

CLOSE THE GAP

1. How does media access impact the reach of a church or ministry? How, specifically, is this

"equation" affecting your organization—or what effects would you like to see in the future?

_____

_____

_____

_____

2. Has your organization considered entering into entertainment-related ventures? Which pursuits would best support the culture, philosophy, and mission of the organization? Explain.

_____

_____

_____

_____

3. Is it best to pursue these ventures under the aegis of the nonprofit corporation? Or should you create a for-profit corporation? Delineate your reasons; be as specific as possible.

_____

_____

_____

_____

4. For your organization, what precautions will be necessary to ensure compliance with IRS rules governing the separation of your business and ministry ventures?

_____

_____

_____

_____

5. Does your organization's employment agreement adequately address the issue of "work made for hire"? How can the agreement be fine-tuned?

_____

_____

_____

_____

6. How has this chapter influenced your approach to business proposals? Are there any current or past deals that look different to you now? Explain.

_____

_____

_____

_____

7. Which of the six testing points of a potential business deal have escaped your attention in the past? Describe the end result *and* the safeguard(s) you will employ for all future opportunities.

_____

_____

_____

_____

Chapter 10

The Power of Partnership

The power of partnership is one of my all-time favorite topics. At TDJ Enterprises, we are able to run a vast business that has interests in areas such as publishing, film, television, the Internet, investments, and the like using an extremely small staff. The reason we are able to do this, very simply, is the power of partnership.

One of the real weaknesses I have observed over the years among many churches, ministries, and other non-profits is that they have an overwhelming tendency to want to do everything on their own. I don't know if this comes from underlying competitive instincts or simply a feeling of, "No one else can do it as well as I can," but the end result is that most of these organizations are in fact missing significant opportunities to benefit their organizations. As your organization begins to understand and embrace the power of partnership, your organization will begin to see the positive results of a number of significant benefits.

———◆·◆·◆———

**Ignoring the power of partnership means
missing significant opportunities and benefits.**

———◆·◆·◆———

THE BENEFITS OF PARTNERSHIP

First, properly utilizing partnerships will allow you to significantly reduce your organization's overhead. As I mentioned above in the comment about TDJ Enterprises, we are able to maintain far-flung business activities with an extremely small staff. We are able to do this and accordingly reduce our overhead because we have engaged in partnerships that allow us to do what we do and allow our partners to do what they do.

With regard to overhead, one common mistake that many churches and ministries make is that, by attempting to do everything themselves, they end up having to support and maintain staff members who are not fully or effectively utilized. For example, if your organization produces and distributes products for sale in retail, it probably does not make sense for you to maintain the full sales staff, not to mention warehousing and shipping capabilities that would be required to handle all of these functions in-house. Instead, it may make more sense to partner with an outside distribution and marketing company that can manage and facilitate these processes for you in exchange for a percentage of the sales.

In addition to pure cost considerations, you also need to consider the quality of the work and services that you'd be receiving. For example, it may make more sense to hire an outside company that has higher expertise and experience in a particular area than your own internal staff might have. Remember, your cost for each employee extends well beyond their salary. You need to consider everything from benefits cost to training cost to the cost to provide office space and other overhead for those employees, as well as the cost and effort involved in managing the employees.

Remember, your cost for each employee extends well beyond salary.

Another benefit that can be obtained from an effective partnership is the ability to leverage your own resources. By not having to utilize your people and funds for activities for which your organization may not be well suited or which another organization can manage more effectively, you are able to free up resources and assets to focus instead on those functions and abilities that go to the core of your mission and for which you do have deep and specific expertise and experience. For example, if you are managing a church and your organization is focused on and all about the Sunday morning experience for your parishioners, you probably don't want to be spending significant time, resources, and effort attempting to manage details such as shipping or managing a call center, which don't relate to what you do well, which is provide a tremendous Sunday morning experience for your worshipers.

Another closely related benefit is that by using partnerships effectively, you are able to focus on what you do well. At the same time, you are able to obtain the benefit of a partner who not only is performing a task or service for which your organization may not be particularly adept but is in fact doing something that that organization is particularly adept and experienced at. In fact, this is what makes the best partnerships. If I am an expert at X and you are an expert at Y, it makes far more sense for us to come together, let me do X, and let you do Y, rather than each trying to perform both functions on our own. All too often the decision to go it on your own, while there may be a business case for it, can lead to a situation where you spend all your time on the half of the equation you are not apt at, and as a result you are ignoring the part of the equation at which you are particularly skilled.

By using partnerships effectively, you will be free to focus on the things you do well.

Here's an example from a significant business organization with which I am familiar. This organization, a national chain of private schools and childcare centers, made repeated attempts over the past couple of years to have their school directors and principals start performing marketing and financial tasks instead of using third parties. The result was this. Rather than spending their time and energy at what they were really good at— namely ensuring that children, parents, and teachers all had a good environment and experience at school—the directors and principals were focused on marketing and financial efforts. Then, because the directors and principals were no longer focused on the customer and the teacher experience and instead were distracted with other matters, the result, quite naturally, was that the customer experience began to suffer. As a result, even though the company thought they were saving money by utilizing the directors rather than the outside marketing and financial staffs, in fact they were hurting their bottom line because they had taken away that very thing that made the school special in the first place—the unique experience and environment that those directors and principals were so skilled at providing on a day-to-day basis to the students and to their parents.

The point is this—you need to focus, pay attention to what it is you do well, and find partners who can focus and spend their energies on what it is that they do well, which is also ideally that same thing that you are not as good at.

**Pay attention to what you do well
and find partners who can focus on
what they do well.**

Another significant benefit of partnerships is that the very existence of a partnership between you and a highly credible third party will give you credibility. For example, TDJ Enterprises is partnered in the movie business with Sony Pictures Entertainment. Because Sony is one of the major studios and has significant credibility in the marketplace, we at TDJ Enterprises now enjoy similar credibility. As a result, we are able to attract better cast and talent to our films because they know we have the strength of our partner behind us. So rather than being one of hundreds of independent producers out there trying to put a film together, we are instead one of a select group of producers who have ongoing relationships with one of the major studios.

WHAT TO LOOK FOR

Now that we've discussed some of the benefits of the power of partnership, let's discuss some of the elements you want to look for when forming quality partnerships for your organization.

The first thing you need to know and remember is that a business partnership is just like any other relationship in your life. Whether it is a relationship with an employer, with your spouse, or with your children, all relationships require an investment of time and effort. In order for the partnership to be as beneficial as possible, each side needs to invest the time to obtain the understanding of the partner. You need to learn and understand both the strengths and the weaknesses of your partner. In addition, you need to understand your partner's motivations. You need to understand what attracted your partner to you. In other words, just as in a marriage, you need to be providing your partner with what they need and they need to be providing you with what you need in order to form a successful relationship.

In addition, as the partnership progresses, you need to be able to maintain a continuous flow of communication and information between the two sides. Just as in any romantic relationship, partners who don't attempt to communicate or understand each other will soon find themselves headed for divorce court.

From a management and leadership standpoint, this means that you need to have a high-level person assigned to each significant partnership or business relationship that your organization has. You have to have someone who is capable, willing, and interested in spending the time and effort that is necessary to maintain and maximize the valued business relationship for your organization. Within TDJ Enterprises, that is my primary role with regard to most of our business partnerships. Both Bishop Jakes and I understand that his schedule is far too tight and he is far too busy to see to and attend to most of the smaller details that are required in maintaining the necessary level of communication with our business partners. As a result, I am the one who makes a conscious effort to spend the time, take the trips, and make the phone calls necessary to make sure that we are adequately investing in all of our business relationships and partnerships.

----●-●-●----

**Find first steps to undertake together before
entering the bigger partner relationship.**

----●-●-●----

The next thing to consider in forming a fruitful partnership, just as in any other romantic relationship, my advice is that you date before you get married. In the business context, what I mean is this. When you are considering entering into a meaningful business relationship with a new partner, find some first steps that you can undertake together before entering into the bigger relationship. Just as with dating, it's not until you actually start spending significant time with someone that you begin to see all of their strengths, weaknesses, and annoying habits, and you will begin to understand just who that person is and whether or not you want to be in a long-term relationship. The same logic applies in the business world. Rather than automatically entering into a five-year exclusive relationship with some business partner, find a first project that you can do together. If that project was successful and the two parties work well together, then it's probably time to consider extending, broadening, or lengthening that relationship so you can have an ongoing flow of business between you.

PLANNING AHEAD

This provides a nice transition into the next point in planning a fruitful business partnership, which is to plan for the end at the beginning. One of my favorite pieces of advice that I have given to clients over the years is that every relationship will come to an end at some point. If it's a marriage between a husband and a wife, either the parties will divorce or at some point one or both of the parties will die. But the end result is the same—at some point, that relationship is going to end.

The same logic applies to the business community. At some point, one party or the other is going to decide that the relationship is no longer beneficial and will move on, or one of the parties is simply going to cease to continue to do business, or some other circumstance will happen. As a result, while the parties and the discussions are firmly at the outset of the relationship, it is always wise to plan for the end of the relationship.

It is always wise to plan for the end of the relationship—at the beginning.

In contracts, this means having the provisions that specify at what time or under what circumstance this business relationship is going to end and what is going to happen with the joint business opportunities when that happens. Oddly enough, it is in success more often than in failure that the breakup of business relationships becomes an issue. Generally speaking, in failure it is usually in the interest of both sides, and therefore not a point of dissention, to end the relationship. However, it is often in success where the parties begin to have differing viewpoints and ideas about how the business should be handled or managed. As a result, it is in these circumstances where you have disputes that could have been avoided by planning on the front end.

The next consideration in planning any significant business relationship is that you need to keep it simple. Frequently, I tell my clients that any business relationship or endeavor should be able to be reduced to a few words and a few pictures on a single piece of paper. Basically, it should come down to, "I'm going to do this, you're going to do that, and we are going to share the risks and rewards of this in a certain manner." While the contracts may become complex after the lawyers become involved, the essence of the business relationship itself should be and needs to be simple and straightforward. If the deal is too complex or if you truly do not understand what it is that you are doing, this is not the right relationship for you and you need to be moving on to other parties.

The essence of the business relationship should be simple and straightforward.

In addition, no matter how big the company is that you are partnering with, remember that you are dealing with the people within that company. This has a couple of important considerations. First, it means that you need to be sure that both the company and the people you will be dealing with are supportive of the partnership. To reach its full potential, any partnership requires champions on both sides.

At TDJ Enterprises, we have a great partnership with Sony Pictures. This partnership works so well because one key executive at Sony is a champion for us. He understands our objectives, and he fights the internal battles to be sure our projects get all that they need.

Every company has its own internal processes and procedures. To succeed in working with the company, you have to have the champion who will make the added effort needed to work the system on your behalf.

A related consideration is—what happens if your champion leaves? Is there sufficient corporate buy-in for your partnership that you can be comfortable that another champion will step up and embrace your deal?

One final note on building successful partnerships, particularly within the context of churches, ministries, and other organizations, is that you need to avoid the wolf in sheep's clothing. Very simply, when people with whom you are trying to do business are spending more time talking about church and God than they are on the subject of the meeting and the business deal at hand, then you might have a problem. While it is natural to discuss items of mutual interest and to attempt to develop a personal relationship with someone, serious business people will always get down to business. All too often, I have seen so-called business people try to impress church leaders with how "spiritual" they are. What they are not doing, however, is showing you what their real life business and experience credentials are.

**Avoid the wolf in sheep's clothing.
Serious business people always get
down to business.**

CLOSE THE GAP

1. Does your organization tend to do everything on its own? What, in your opinion, underlies this tendency? How can addressing the issue free up your organization to better fulfill its mission?

_____

_____

_____

_____

2. Consider the potential of partnerships to reduce your organization's overhead. How can you/your leader and the executive staff better define this potential benefit and develop a plan of action to appropriate it?

_____

_____

_____

_____

3. How can you more clearly differentiate between what your organization does well and what a partner would do better? How will this serve to preserve your brand?

_____

_____

_____

_____

4. Which specific partnerships would help to elevate
    your organization's credibility in a particular field
    of endeavor? What facts inform your opinion?

_____

_____

_____

_____

5. What strengths, weaknesses, motivations, and
    needs have you uncovered in regard to a current
    or potential partner? How might you initiate a
    "dating" relationship with a prospective partner?

_____

_____

_____

_____

6. Do you have a plan for the eventual end of a cur-
    rent partnership? What is the plan? What steps
    can you take to ensure that you enter your next
    partnership with a good plan for its ending?

_____

_____

_____

_____

7. Which of your business relationships are simple
    and straightforward? Which are overly compli-
    cated? How are these qualities affecting outcomes?
    Who are your "champions" in each case, and how
    might their departures affect your relationships
    with their respective organizations?

_____

_____

_____

_____

A Parting Thought

Over the last few decades, we have embarked on a new era in the world of ministry. We now have mega-churches and other equally large para-church and ministry organizations. As we have discussed, these organizations require a level of management and business expertise that was not required only a short time ago.

One issue with the mega-church era that is only now beginning to come to the forefront is succession planning. In the past, it was a relatively simple matter to replace a church leader. Either the denomination sent in someone new or the church board found a new pastor.

However, that process is not nearly as easy in the age of the mega-church. What do you do when the pastor of a 30,000-member church either dies or retires? Not many people can even begin to think about taking over such a large organization. At the same time, more and more pastors are getting burned out and are looking for an exit strategy.

This means that the existing pastor/leader (who built the organization) has to be aware of this issue and take active steps to develop potential replacements and put a plan in place. We cannot let these churches die for lack of planning.

The best advice that I can give on this issue is to simply think about it and start considering the options.

About Curtis Wallace

M r. Wallace utilizes his unique combination of business and legal experience along with his in-depth knowledge of the faith-based/nonprofit world to guide clients who are navigating the intersection of faith and business. His expertise includes organizational structure, ventures between nonprofit and for-profit entities, entertainment, publishing, real estate matters, financing, and crisis management.

Mr. Wallace is a lawyer and currently serves as the Chief Operating Officer/General Counsel of TDJ Enterprises, LLP. In these capacities, Mr. Wallace works to bring the worlds of faith and business together for the mutual benefit of both.

During his tenure, Mr. Wallace has developed and overseen partnerships with entities including:

- Film production venture with Sony Pictures Entertainment
- Publishing joint venture with Simon and Schuster (Atria Imprint)
- Television and film joint venture with Codeblack Entertainment

- Nationally syndicated radio program with Radio One/Syndication One

Mr. Wallace has served as the producer or executive in charge (on behalf of TDJE/New Dimensions Entertainment) of the following projects:

- The live stage productions Woman Thou Art Loosed, Behind Closed Doors, and Cover Girls
- The feature films Woman Thou Art Loosed (starring Kimberly Elise, released in 2004 by Magnolia Films, and winner of Best American Film at the 2004 Santa Barbara International Film Festival), Not Easily Broken (starring Morris Chestnut and Taraji P. Henson, released in 2009 by Sony/Tristar), Jumping the Broom (currently in production and scheduled for a May 6, 2011 release by Sony Pictures), and On the Seventh Day, a Woman Thou Art Loosed Film (currently in pre-production and scheduled to start filming in late 2010 for a 2011 release on television and DVD)
- Sitcom T.D. Jakes' One Love (starring Mark Curry), scheduled for a summer 2011 release
- "Maximize the Moment" infomercial with Time Life Video
- The creation and touring of the God's Leading Ladies conference series
- Multiple music projects released under the Dexterity Sounds label, currently in partnership with Universal Music

Mr. Wallace also works closely with The Potter's House of Dallas, Inc. (founded by Bishop T.D. Jakes) on business, transactional, and IRS compliance matters. Mr. Wallace is also a frequent advisor to nonprofit organizations, as well as a speaker on business, nonprofit, and leadership issues.

In addition to the foregoing, Mr. Wallace serves on the board of directors of BN Media Holdings, which owns both Affinity 4, an affinity marketing company that has helped nonprofits raise over $76 million to date, and beliefnet.com, the largest website in the spirituality category.

From a community standpoint, Mr. Wallace has previously served on the board of directors of the Parkland Foundation as well as Wycliffe Resources, Inc. Mr. Wallace continues to serve on the Dallas County Blue Ribbon Commission for Parkland Hospital, a group responsible for leading the effort to construct a new $1.2 billion public hospital for the citizens of Dallas.

Prior to joining TDJ Enterprises, Mr. Wallace practiced law, first with Weil, Gotshal & Manges, and later with the firm of Brewer, Brewer, Anthony & Middlebrook, where he headed the firm's transactional practice group. In his legal practice, Mr. Wallace represented individuals, businesses, banks, investment groups, and nonprofit organizations in a diverse array of corporate and real estate transactions ranging from mergers and acquisitions to financing to real estate leases, purchases, and sales.

Mr. Wallace lives in Keller, Texas, with his wife, Julaina, and three sons, Jackson, Harrison, and Carter, and his daughter Caroline.

In the right hands, This Book will Change Lives!

Most of the people who need this message will not be looking for this book. To change their lives, you need to put a copy of this book in their hands.

> *But others (seeds) fell into good ground, and brought forth fruit, some a hundred-fold, some sixty-fold, some thirty-fold* (Matthew 13:8).

Our ministry is constantly seeking methods to find the good ground, the people who need this anointed message to change their lives. Will you help us reach these people?

> *Remember this—a farmer who plants only a few seeds will get a small crop. But the one who plants generously will get a generous crop* (2 Corinthians 9:6).

EXTEND THIS MINISTRY BY SOWING
3 BOOKS, 5 BOOKS, 10 BOOKS, OR MORE TODAY,
AND BECOME A LIFE CHANGER!

Thank you,

Don Nori Sr., Founder
Destiny Image
Since 1982